SURVIVE

an
Active Shooter

Awareness, Preparedness, and Responses for Extreme Violence

David Fowler

Founder and Author of AVADE®
Workplace Violence Training
Programs

WORKPLACE VIOLENCE PREVENTION

SURVIVE an Active Shooter
Awareness, Preparedness, and Responses
for Extreme Violence

Published by Personal Safety Training, Inc.
P.O. Box 2957, Coeur d' Alene, ID 83816
(208) 664-5551

ISBN: **978-1537185286**

Personal Safety Training Inc.
Telephone: (208) 691-7481

www.AVADEtraining.com
www.PersonalSafetyTraining.com

Also, by David Fowler
Violence In The Workplace, Violence in the Workplace II, Violence in the Workplace III, Be Safe Not Sorry, and To Serve and Protect

DISCLAIMER

Neither the author nor the publisher, Personal Safety Training, Inc., dictates policies or procedures for the use of any violence prevention, self-defense, or any physical intervention authorized for use by a depart- ment/agency or private individual. The suggestions/op- tions disseminated in this book are simply that, sugges- tions or options. Each individual, department or agency is responsible for developing their own "policies and pro- cedures" regarding the use of violence prevention, self-defense, and physical intervention for their personnel and for themselves. Although every effort has been made for this book to be complete and accurate, it is im- possible to predict, discuss or plan for every circum- stance or situation which might arise in the course of de- fending yourself and any contact with a violent or ag- gressive person(s) or during a crime. Every reader must always take into consideration their experience, physical abilities, professional responsibilities, agency and de- partment procedures, and state, local, and federal legal requirements. With this in mind, each reader must eval- uate the recommendations and techniques contained in this book and decide for himself (herself) which should be used and under what circumstances. Each reader assumes the risk of loss, injury, and damages associated with this book and the use of the information obtained in it. The author and publisher, Personal Safety Training, Inc., cannot guarantee or warrant the legal, medical, tactical, or technical suggestions/options in this book. **ANY IMPLIED WARRANTIES ARE EXPRESSLY DISAVOWED.**

DEDICATION

To the Victims and Family and Friends of Victims:

With a sad heart and righteous indignation, I write this book. Too many have lost their lives and had their destinies stolen be- cause of extreme violence. The world around us continues to change, and in many cases, not for the better. My hope is for people to learn and apply the strategies and techniques in this book to survive an Active Shooter. I endeavor to help people live a safe and productive life, full of peace, harmony, and free will. My intention for the reader of this book is to have a plan for extreme violence. As the old saying goes, "He who fails to plan, plans to fail." With a plan, we can respond; without a plan, we become victims. That just doesn't work for me! The trumpet must be sounded for the times we are in. From the book of Ezekiel 33:2-6, "Son of man, speak to the sons of your people and say to them, 'If I bring a sword upon a land, and the people of the land take one man from among them and make him their watchman, and he sees the sword coming upon the land and blows on the trumpet and warns the people, then he who hears the sound of the trumpet and does not take warning, and a sword comes and takes him away, his blood will be on his own head."

As a Watchman for YOUR Safety,

David Fowler
David Fowler

ACKNOWLEDGEMENTS

First and foremost, I thank God that he has given me the skills and talents to help people be safe. Without Him, I can do nothing. "Greater love has no one than this, than to lay down one's life for his friends." John 15:13 (NKJV)

I would also like to thank all the organizations (managers, directors, supervisors, and bosses) that I have worked with over the last couple of decades that have put their trust and confidence in me to provide violence prevention training to their staff. A special thanks to their staff too. Many of you were mandated to at- tend our safety training on violence. Your feedback has inspired us to keep doing what we are doing.

Special thanks to the following individuals for their support and technical advice: Steve Baker, Genelle Fowler, Dennis Fivecoat, Patrick Gibney, Jamie Lang, and Chris Turner. Your wisdom and inspiration echo through these pages.

I would also like to thank my children for their positive support throughout all of the travel teaching violence prevention throughout the US: My daughters, Kaley, Hannah, and Jacquelyn; sons, Shane and Aaron; and grandchildren, Carter and Wren.

For all of you who have prayed for us in our safety ministry in the secular – thank YOU!

Every book, every training program, and every day on the road teaching and preaching the message of safety wouldn't be possible without my bride: Genelle Fowler. Thank you, I need you and love you with all that I am.

CONTENTS

INTRODUCTION 1

CHAPTER 1 10
Active Shooter Awareness

CHAPTER 2 21
Don't Give Them Any Honor!

CHAPTER 3 26
What We Know about Active Shooters

CHAPTER 4 38
Vigilance for Violence

CHAPTER 5 45
Who Commits Violence?

CHAPTER 6 56
YOU Have the Right to Defend Yourself!

CHAPTER 7 62
The Stress Continuum

CHAPTER 8 69
Escape-Escape-Escape

CHAPTER 9 75
Hide, Call, Lock, and Barricade

CHAPTER 10 86
Attack the Attacker

CHAPTER 11 95
Law Enforcement, Post Incident Responses & Documentation

CHAPTER 12 103
Stop the Bleed

CONTENTS

CHAPTER 13 ....*109*
Honoring the Victims and Heroes

ABOUT THE AUTHOR *117*

BIBLIOGRAPHY/REFERENCE...*119*

ACTIVE SHOOTER POSTERS *125*

TRAINING COURSES FOR YOU AND YOUR AGENCY *127*

INTRODUCTION

Word of Caution. For many people, the topic of violence, active shooter, and especially extreme violence can invoke a myriad of stress responses. It is not the author's or publisher's intention to add to any person's trauma, stress, or any medical, physical, emotional, or psychological condition. It is, however, our intention to help people Be Safe. Following are some important facts regarding extreme violence and active shooters.

Incidents of an Active Shooter or mass-type killings have been happening here in the US and in a number of other countries for many years. This is not a new phenomenon. What is new is the number of incidents we are seeing and the increase in the loss of life in these horrendous acts of violence. America has now witnessed the worst modern mass shootings in our history.

- Pulse nightclub, Orlando, FL
  June 12th, 2016 - 49 deaths, 53 injured

- First Baptist Church, Sutherland Springs, TX
  Novem- ber 5th, 2017 – 27 deaths, 20 injured

- Route 91 Harvest Festival, Las Vegas, NV
  October 1st, 2017 – 58 deaths, 527+ injured

Active Shooter training is just one piece of an effective work-place violence prevention plan. Violence in the workplace hap- pens every second, minute, and hour of each day in the United States. Fortunately, incidents of an Active Shooter are not even remotely that prevalent. However, we must be prepared for this type of extreme violence.

The AVADE® Active Shooter Training Program and Training books are designed to increase your awareness, preparedness, and responses for Extreme Violence.

The AVADE® Active Shooter training program is an integral component in meeting the requirements of State and Federal guidelines, as well as OSHA's General Duty Clause, to provide employees with a workplace free from recognized hazards.

An employer's overall plan should include administrative, behavioral, and environmental strategies to prevent and mitigate the risk of workplace violence and an active shooter incident.

The AVADE® Active Shooter Training Course provides this level of education and will also empower you to:

- Identify, prevent, and respond to an active shooter incident/event.

- Learn universal precautions against violence by applying the principles of the AVADE® Active Shooter training program.

- Learn the characteristics of violent individuals who commit acts of extreme violence.

- Enhance your safety by understanding the rules for surviving an active shooter.

- Learn the predicting factors of aggression and violence in the workplace and how they may be related to an individual that could commit an extreme act of violence.

- Learn strategies to avoid physical harm by applying the principles of time and distance.

The **AVADE® Active Shooter Training Program** was researched and developed to be the most complete and effective active shooter training program for the corporate environment.

The AVADE® Active Shooter Training Program is tailored specifically to the unique needs and dynamics of the workplace.

Active Shooter Awareness

Do YOU Know…

- **What you would do in an active shooter incident?**

- **What your policies and procedures are for an active shooter situation?**

- **What the chances are of this type of incident happening?**

- **Where your escape route is right now?**

- **What you would do if you didn't have an escape route?**

- **How to notify help during an active shooter incident?**

- **What to do after an incident has occurred?**

Is an Active Shooter Workplace Violence? _____

Workplace Violence Defined

Workplace violence is any act of aggression, verbal assault, physical assault, or threatening behavior that occurs in the workplace environment and causes physical or emotional harm to customers (patients), staff, or visitors.

Violence in the workplace is compromised of many categories, from verbal harassment, intimidation, threatening behavior, obscene phone calls, property damage, robbery, bomb threats, verbal assault, suicide, stalking, road rage, gang violence, physical assault, sexual assault, edged weapons, guns, hostage/kidnapping, terrorism, and active shooter incidents/events.

Have you experienced any of the above? Most of us have.

The AVADE® WPV Prevention training programs meet the requirements of State and Federal guidelines as well as OSHA's General Duty Clause to provide employees with a workplace free from recognized hazards likely to cause death or serious physical harm. The AVADE® Workplace Violence (WPV) Prevention Training Program was researched and developed to be the most comprehensive, complete, and effective workplace violence prevention training program for the corporate and healthcare environment.

OSHA General Duty Clause: The Occupational Safety and Health Act of 1970 (OSH Act)1 mandates that, in addition to compliance with hazard-specific standards, all employers have a general duty to provide their employees with a workplace free from recognized hazards likely to cause death or serious physical harm.

The **AVADE® WPV Prevention Training Programs** are tailored specifically to the unique needs and dynamics of the workplace. These unique dynamics include preparing for an active shooter. This book will not cover all the categories of workplace violence. It is designed to specifically cover the Active Shooter category.

AVADE® Principles for Surviving an Active Shooter:

A = Awareness

V = Vigilance

A = Avoidance

D = Defense

E = Escape/Environment

The AVADE® philosophy incorporates learning new habits, skills, and actions that employers and employees can use to enhance their personal safety and their ability to defend themselves or others from dangerous situations, crime, and violence.

AVADE® workplace violence prevention has been taught in private corporations, healthcare agencies, schools, community programs, and civic institutions for many years. The founder of the AVADE® Training programs, David Fowler, has over thirty years' experience and has made personal safety training his life's work. He has an extensive background in training, martial science, and all functions of security management and operations. He is also the author of Be Safe Not Sorry: The Art and Science of Keeping You and Your Family Safe from Crime and Violence, available on amazon.com and at his websites:

- **www.personalsafetytraining.com**
- **www.avadetraining.com**

"The overall vision and philosophy of the AVADE® Training programs are the moral essence of life itself; to live a safe and positive life with peace, security, harmony, and freedom of choice."

The AVADE® Workplace Violence Prevention training programs are designed to educate, prevent, and mitigate the risk of violence to individuals in the workplace. One aspect of preventing and mitigating violence in the workplace is preventing and responding to an incident of extreme violence (Active Shooter).

The AVADE® Active Shooter Training is comprised of three training levels:

Level I – Awareness-Preparedness-Responses for Extreme Violence
Level II – Active Shooter Strategies and Skills Drills
Level III – Active Shooter Simulation Drills

Awareness-Preparedness-Responses for Extreme Violence (Active Shooter)

- Active Shooter Awareness

- Don't Give Them Any Honor!

- What We Know about Active Shooters

- Vigilance for Violence

- Who Commits Violence?

- YOU Have the Right to Defend Yourself!

- The Stress Continuum

- Escape-Escape-Escape

- HIDE, Call, and Barricade

- Attack (FIGHT) the Attacker

- Law Enforcement, Post-Incident Responses/Documentation

- Stop the Bleed

- Honoring the Victims and Heroes

Level II Active Shooter Strategies / Skills Drills

- Strategies / Skills Drills for Escaping (RUN)
- Strategies / Skills Drills for Hiding and Covering
- Strategies / Skills Drills for Alerting (911)
- Strategies / Skills Drills for Locking-Barricading
- Strategies / Skills Drills for Attacking the Attacker
- Strategies / Skills Drills for Stopping the Bleed

Level III Active Shooter Simulation Drills

- Simulation Drill Objectives
- Simulation Pre-Event Planning
- Simulation Drill Overview
- Simulation Safety Rules
- Simulation Scenarios #1 and #2
- Pre-Event Survey
- Day of Event CheckList
- Defined Staff Roles for Active Shooter Simulation

Special Note: Simulation training involves preplanning and on-site staff involvement. AVADE® will assist the agency with preplanning arrangements and coordination. An agency MUST be proactively involved in preplanning for simulation learning.

AVADE® Active Shooter (Awareness, Preparedness & Responses for Extreme Violence) involves scenario-based exercises, group interaction, discussion, and lecture. AVADE® training offers three certifications that can be adapted into a variety of scheduling and training dynamics.

- AVADE® Level I Active Shooter (2-hour) certification
- AVADE® Level II Active Shooter (4-hour) certification
- AVADE® Level III Active Shooter (1-day) certification

Special Note: this book specifically focuses on Level I. Please contact AVADE® for basic and instructor training certifications.

The expression **"Active Shooter"** and **"Run-Hide-Fight"** have become regular terms in our vernacular. Our children are taught lock-down drills in our school system because of Active Shooter incidents that have plagued our country. Many com- panies today have policies and procedures for Active Shooter events. More and more people are waking up to the reality that we need to know how to recognize, respond to, and prevent acts of extreme violence in our workplaces and communities.

AVADE® Active Shooter is Evidenced-Based Training

Research from the FBI, DHS, FEMA, OSHA, IAHSS, DOJ, Secret Service, WPV Laws, Department of Labor & Industries, The Run-Hide-Fight Campaign, Stop the Bleed, AVADE® Workplace Violence Prevention Programs, and more...

Benefits of AVADE® Training for Active Shooter:

- Increased Awareness
- Increased Confidence
- Increased Overall Safety
- Increased Quality of Life
- Increased Self-Improvement
- Increased Overall Sense of Peace
- Increased Ability to Protect Others
- Increase Ability to Respond to Situations

You will also experience:

- Reduced Fear
- Reduced Stress
- Reduced Injuries
- Reduced Liability Risk
- Reduced Loss of Property
- Reduced Feelings of Inadequacy

After going through **AVADE® Active Shooter Training: Awareness, Preparedness & Responses for Extreme Violence**, refer back to this book as your personal refresher course.

This book, Survive an Active Shooter, will help remind you how to survive and escape a violent attack and much-much more. ***Read and study carefully***. Integrate the lessons you learn here. Unfortunately, one day you may be responsible for saving your own life—and the lives of your co-workers.

Chapter 1

Active Shooter Awareness

Surviving an active shooter begins with Awareness. People have perished because they lack awareness of what to do in an active shooter situation. The goal of this chapter is to help you understand what awareness is and how you can increase yours. There are many levels of awareness, and we will briefly look at them and why they are important to your safety in an active shooter situation. More and more people are waking up to the reality that we need to know how to recognize, respond to, and prevent acts of extreme violence in our workplaces and communities.

Awareness is defined as: *A mental state or ability to perceive, feel, or be conscious of people, emotions, conditions, events, objects, and patterns.*

- The key to awareness is knowledge and understanding.
- The gift of this awareness is wisdom.
- Change your awareness, and you can change your life!

A person's awareness can range from being completely unaware to a hyper state of awareness. Both extremes can be dangerous. A calm, vigilant state of awareness can save your life and the life of others. Are you aware of what an Active Shooter is?

Active Shooter Defined

The FBI defines an active shooter as one or more individuals actively engaged in killing or attempting to kill people in a populated area. Implicit in this definition is the shooter's use of one or more firearms.

Noun: A person who is presently using a gun to shoot people in a confined and populated area.[1]

Active Shooters are also known as (AKA):

- Extreme Violence
- Terrorist
- Mass Killer
- Spree Killer
- Active Killer
- Mass Murderer
- Violent Intruder
- Radical Extremist
- Active Assailant
- Mass Attacker

Even though there are many names for an Active Shooter, we will utilize the term "Active Shooter" throughout this book. Regardless of what we call them, they all have this in common—a desire to kill innocent people.

Mass Murder / Mass Killer-Shooter / Mass Attacks

Mass Murder

- FOUR or more <u>killed</u> in a single incident/event, at the same general time and location, not including the shooter.

---

[1] https://www.dictionary.com/browse/active-shooter

Mass Shooting

- FOUR or more <u>shot-injured and/or killed</u> in a single incident/event, at the same general time and location, not including the shooter.[2]

Mass Attacks

- THREE or more <u>shot-injured and/or killed</u> in a single incident/event at the same general time and location, not including the shooter

- A mass shooting/attack is an incident involving multiple victims of gun violence. There is no widely accepted definition of the term mass shooting/attack.

- Based on this, it is generally agreed that a mass shooting is whenever three or more people are shot (injured or killed), not including the shooters.

- Gun Violence Archive[3] defines a "mass shooting" as "four or more shot (injured or killed) in a single incident, at the same general time and location, not including the shooter," differentiating between a mass shooting and mass murder and not counting shooters as victims.

- The United States' Congressional Research Service acknowledges that there is not a broadly accepted definition and defines a "public mass shooting" as an event where someone selects four or more people and shoots them with firearms in an indiscriminate manner, echoing the FBI's definition of the term "mass murder," but adding the indiscriminate factor.[4]

---

[2] https://www.gunviolencearchive.org/methodology

[4] https://en.wikipedia.org/wiki/Mass_shooting

Proactive Response Planning = Prevention / Intervention

Proactive vs. Reactive: Prevention and intervention are essential to eliminating and mitigating risks in the workplace. Employers now recognize the importance of being proactive in their implementation of workplace violence policies and procedures, conducting worksite audits/analysis, tracking and trending incidents, training and  educating staff, as well as implementing proactive measures to reduce the risk of violence to guests, staff, clients, and visitors. A well-thought-out plan for the prevention of workplace violence involves a proactive response versus an after-the-fact, reactive-driven response.

Situational Awareness

What would YOU do if you just became aware of this in your environment?

–That is a GUN being pointed at YOU!

Some people will say…

- "I would freeze."
- "I would yell and scream."
- "I would give my money to them."
- "I wouldn't know what to do."

"People will answer the question differently based on their level of situational awareness."

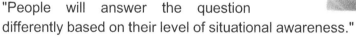

Situational Awareness

Situational awareness means being aware of what is happen- ing around you. It means understanding how information, inci- dents, and your own actions will affect your goals and objectives, both now and in the near future. Inadequate situational awareness has been identified as one of the primary factors in accidents attributed to human error.

Situational Awareness is best explained in a simple equation:

I_____ + R_____ = O_____

If an individual pulls out a gun and begins shooting (*incident*), knowing how to respond (*response*) to the situation can lead you to creating distance from the attacker (*outcome*).

By taking responsibility for all the situations you are in, you can increase your personal safety, by making conscious, informed choices and decisions about your environments, the people around you, and the places you frequent.

Each person carries a three-fold response-ability.

1. Learn the signs of a potentially volatile situation and ways to prevent an incident.

2. Learn the best steps for survival when faced with an active shooter situation.

3. Be prepared to work with law enforcement during the response.

Increase your Situational Awareness of HOW to respond to an Active Shooter.

There are only two effective **Responses to Active Shooter**.

1. Armed Response = Law Enforcement / Armed Security

2. Unarmed Response = Escape!

Understanding that there are only two appropriate responses to an active shooter incident is crucial. A person that is intent on killing others will do so to those that are frozen/not moving, submissive, pleading, and to those that don't know what to do. The AVADE® Active Shooter training offers options-based responses. The best option/response for most of us to survive an active shooter is to escape if safe to do so. The following information will outline the rules for surviving an active shooter if escape is possible or if it is not possible.

A Special Note for individuals who are licensed to carry a firearm for work or personal. An appropriate lawful decision/response for engaging an active shooter MUST be adhered to. More on this in the module on Attack the Attacker.

"He who fails to plan, plans to fail." – Benjamin Franklin

Now, what would YOU do if you just became aware of this in your environment?

Time & Distance = Safety (**RUN!**)
- Best Answer!

The concept of time or distance illustrates that having time or distance can give us distance or time from a violent person, place, event, or thing.

What we do with our time can be the most precious investment we ever make.

"See Gun- RUN!, Hear Gun- RUN!"
– David Fowler, author of AVADE® Workplace Violence Prevention

Reaction Time = OODA Loop
Air Force Colonel John Boyd coined the term "OODA Loop" to describe a form of reaction time and decision-making.

OODA stands for observe-orient-decide-act.

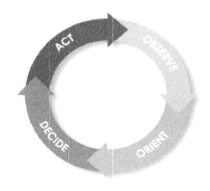

Boyd's key concept is that the decision cycle is the process by which an individual reacts to an event. Accordingly, the key to victory is to be able to create situations wherein one can make appropriate decisions more quickly than one's opponent. This was originally a theory of achieving success in air-to-air combat.

Time is the dominant parameter in the OODA Loop.

The individual who goes through the OODA Loop in the shortest time prevails, because his opponent is caught responding to situations that have already changed.

- **Observation**
  The collection of relevant data through your senses.

- **Orientation**
  The analysis of observed data to form your current mental perspective of what is happening.

- **Decision**
  Determining a course of action based on your current mental perspective.

- **Action**
  The physical acting-out of your decisions.

When it's between you and the active shooter, the individual who goes through the OODA Loop in the shortest time prevails, because his opponent is caught responding to situations that have already changed. Your ability to OODA during an active shooter incident can save your life!

Awareness to Survive an Active Shooter Incident

- **To Survive an Active Shooter, YOU must understand the RULES for Surviving an Active Shooter.**

- **The following rules will help you Develop & Increase YOUR Awareness of how to Survive an Active Shooter Incident**

  1. Escape (RUN) if safe to do so!

  2. HIDE and cover in place if you cannot escape. (SAFE ROOM)

  3. Alert (911) authorities—police, armed security.

  4. Lock doors in your immediate area.

  5. Place barriers and remain absolutely quiet.

  6. If escape is not possible and danger is imminent, attack (FIGHT) the attacker.

  7. When law enforcement arrives, be submissive, expose your palms, and do what they tell you to do.

The **seven rules for surviving an active shooter** will be unpacked throughout the remainder of this book. The above rules/principles are an expanded understanding of the fundamentals of run-hide-fight.

In a violent incident, the most important aspect of survival will be your mental strength and ability (awareness) to respond effectively and appropriately to save your life and potentially the lives of others. Preplanning for an active shooter incident creates a proactive and responsive mindset.

Developing & Increasing YOUR Awareness to Survive an Active Shooter Incident: Developing and increasing your awareness does not mean becoming paranoid or hyper-vigilant. It simply means using all your senses.

There are several ways to improve and increase your responses and awareness of an Active Shooter situation.

Planning and preparing for situations that haven't happened yet. This is done by pre-playing (mental movies) what you would do if faced with a crisis situation.

Being Responsible or "Response-able" is the ability to choose your awareness, responses, and attitude towards incidents, yourself, and others.

Pay Attention to what is going on inside of you and outside of you.

Be Present. You don't have to keep your mind constantly busy thinking about all the possible things that can go amiss. Being present or in the moment allows your awareness to be at its most optimal state.

Be Proactive. Recognize the importance of responsibility and awareness. Proactive people don't blame circumstances or conditions for their behavior or outcomes. Their behavior and outcomes are a product of their own conscious choices, based on their knowledge and values rather than their circum- stances.

Attitude Is Everything. Your success with everything you do depends on your attitude. Creating a positive attitude about life and all of the events you will experience will help develop and enhance your awareness.

Awareness is always the beginning of everything. Right now, you can make a conscious decision to be aware of your surroundings, your responses, your environment, and your mental state. **Awareness is a choice.**

Chapter 2

Don't Give Them Any Honor!

Why would we give honor to insane people who are killing unarmed innocent people? Using their name and comparing them to others creates stardom of infamy that needs to STOP! Many in the media have taken this stance as well. And, of course, the shame and humiliation that the killer's family experienced from their insanity (the shooter) are unimaginable.

Don't Give Them Any Honor!

A part of understanding and responding to an active shooter incident is to be aware of how we report and discuss such incidents. Using the name of the active shooter killers and comparing them to others creates stardom of infamy and may encourage other would-be killers.

- Some shooters are motivated by a desire for fame, notoriety, and/or recognition.

- When the media focuses on the shooter, they provide this fame, notoriety, and recognition.

- This focus allows the shooter to accomplish one of his goals and validates his life and actions.

- Media coverage can create a contagion effect producing more shootings.

- Some shootings may be prevented by removing one of the incentives.

- We encourage the media and others not to name the shooters or focus on their lives.

- The shooters should be as unrecognized in their deaths as they were in their lives.

- Media coverage should focus on the victims and the heroes.

http://www.dontnamethem.org/

What do they all have in common?

What they all have in common:
They all have crazy eyes; they are all cowards, and they all had delusional ideas, they all have a mental illness, they all heard demonic voices, and they all killed a lot of innocent people.

The Sandy Hook Elementary School shooting occurred on December 14, 2012, in Newtown, Connecticut, when a 20-year-old killer fatally shot 20 children aged between 6 and 7 years old, as well as six adult staff members. Prior to driving to the school, the perpetrator shot and killed his mother at their Newtown home. As first responders arrived at the scene, the shooter committed suicide by shooting himself in the head.

The Virginia Tech shooting, also known as the Virginia Tech massacre, occurred on April 16, 2007, on the campus of Virginia Polytechnic Institute and State University in Blacksburg, Virginia.

SURVIVE AN ACTIVE SHOOTER

A student at Virginia Tech shot and killed 32 people and wounded 17 others in two separate attacks (another six people were injured escaping from classroom windows), approximately two hours apart, before committing suicide. To date, this was the worst school shooting in U.S. history.

Century 16 Movie Theater in Aurora, Colorado, July 20, 2012, a mass shooting occurred during a midnight screening of the film *The Dark Knight Rises*. A gunman, dressed in tactical clothing, set off tear gas grenades and shot into the audience with multiple firearms. Twelve people were killed, and seventy others were injured. The sole assailant was arrested in his car parked outside the cinema minutes later. Prior to the shooting, he rigged his apartment with homemade explosives, which were defused by a bomb squad the day after the shooting.

U.S. Representative Gabrielle Gifford and eighteen others were shot during a constituent meeting held in a supermarket parking lot in Tucson, AZ, on January 8, 2011. Six people died, including a nine-year-old girl, Christina-Taylor Green. Gifford was holding the meeting, called "Congress on Your Corner," in the parking lot of a Safeway store when the shooter drew a pistol and shot her in the head before proceeding to fire on other people.

Active Shooters have a thing or two in common.

Among their similarities:

- A lone wolf personality. They are socially isolated, generally having few if any friends.

- Situational events in their lives have led them to become despondent and often depressed.

- They have feelings of alienation, bullying, and persecution and tend to blame others for their problems.

- These are individuals who are angry enough to kill their family members or coworkers, or classmates.

- They've had very little interaction with police or mental health providers.

- They are nontraditional criminals, and they fear detection unless there is a suicide component to their plan.

- As their world starts to unravel, they formulate a plan to target their persecutors.

- There is generally a loss that precipitates the attack, and they have no place to turn for help when they get into trouble.

- They pick high-volume places to carry out their plan.

- They identify a place that has a high volume of people with little police presence.

Massachusetts State Police officer Todd McGhee: http://www.po-licemag.com/blog/swat/story/2012/08/profile-of-an-active-shooter.aspx

The following pictures are NOT to promote or sensationalize these killers whatsoever.

These killers are cowards!

These pictures only represent a strategy of warfare – know your enemy!

"If you know the enemy and know yourself, you need not fear the result of a hundred battles. If you know yourself but not the enemy, for every victory gained, you will also suffer a defeat. If you know neither the enemy nor yourself, you will succumb in every battle." — *Sun Tzu*, *The Art of War*

Chapter 3

What We Know About Active Shooters

One of the most extreme incidences of violence in today's society is an active shooter incident/event. Extreme violence in the workplace/society may include acts of terrorism, active shooters, serial rapists, serial killers, sociopaths, and psychopaths.

Extreme violence goes beyond our human understanding of how and why members of the same species can inflict such pain and harm on one another.

- **Terrorism:** the use of violence or the threat of violence, especially against civilians, in the pursuit of political or religious goals.

- **Active Shooters:** one or more individuals actively engaged in killing or attempting to kill people in a populated area. Implicit in this definition is the shooter's use of one or more firearms.

- **Serial Rapist:** a person who forces a series of victims into unwanted sexual activity.

- **Serial Killers:** a person who murders three or more people, usually in service of abnormal psychological gratification.

- **Sociopaths:** a person with a personality disorder manifesting itself in extreme antisocial attitudes and behavior with a lack of conscience.

- **Psychopaths:** a person suffering from a chronic mental disorder with abnormal or violent social behavior.

Active Shooter incidents take place in many environments. Most people, when they hear the term active shooter, they think of their workplace or where their children go to school. However, active shooter incidents take place in a variety of environments.

How many of the following environments will you be in, in your lifetime? Environmental Awareness for Active Shooter Incidents (How many will you be in?)

- Malls
- Schools
- Casinos
- Hospitals
- Churches
- Restaurants
- Medical Clinics
- Movie Theaters
- Military Installations
- Government Buildings
- Retail Shops / Stores, etc.

According to a recent (FBI) Federal Bureau of Investigation study where 250 active shooter incidents took place in the United States. They discovered that the location categories and percentage of incidents were as follows:

- 42% took place in areas of commerce/business

- 21% took place in educational environments

- 10% took place on government properties

- 14% took place in open spaces

- 5% took place in residences

- 4% took place in houses of worship

- 4% percent took place in healthcare environments

Overall, your chances of being involved in an active shooter incident is fairly low. However, our odds of encountering an attacker may increase as we are in a variety of environments throughout our lifetime.

Environmental Awareness = 360-Degree

It is your ability to understand and recognize the many factors relating to your environment and how they can benefit you or limit you. When you are aware of what is going on in your environment, you are more capable and able to respond effectively and appropriately, using your OODA reaction time to its fullest.

Environmental awareness is the ability to understand and recognize the many factors relating to your environment and how they can benefit you or limit you. This is very important for surviving an active shooter incident.

Creating a constant Awareness of what is around you is described as a 360-degree environmental awareness.

- We use our 360-degree view of awareness in our vehicles every day that we drive.

- We know for certain that this awareness keeps us safe.

- Why not use your 360-degree awareness outside of your vehicle too.

- What is around us, above us, and below us may be a threat? Be Aware!

Risk Factors to Violence (Person(s) of Concern)

History of Violence
The best predictor of future violence in many cases is past violence. Past violence might not be indicated in a criminal history report, so it is important to cover this in interviews, social media reviews, personnel file reviews, or other available sources.

Childhood Exposure to Violence
Violence in a person of concern's family of origin or adolescent peer group has also been identified as a risk factor for adult violence.

Substance Abuse or Dependence
Psychostimulants are a concern and are encountered as both illicit and prescription drugs; they can increase the fight or flight response, and more importantly, for targeted violence assessment, they can cause grandiosity and/or paranoia in some. Generally, prescription medication side effects are variable and can sometimes include violent ideation and altered thought processing. Alcohol lowers serotonin levels in the brain, potentially leading to irritability and aggression. The use of non-prescription substances could be evidence of self-there is evidence that drug and alcohol abuse is significantly lower among those engaged in targeted violence than those engaged in impulsive/reactive violence.

Personality Disturbance or Disorder
Paranoia, narcissism, borderline personality, psychopathic or significant antisocial tendencies, or significant and sustained anger manifestations, can all increase the risk of targeted violence and should be taken seriously. They can cause a person of concern to believe violence is justified and acceptable.

Organized

If a person of concern has a demonstrated ability to organize behavior, regardless of any superficial appearance of illogical or incoherent speech or personal presentation, then he is potentially able to plan and carry out an act of violence.

Severe Mental Illness

Severe mental illness slightly increases the risk of general violence toward others. Psychosis, in particular, can raise concerns depending upon the nature of the symptoms; however, psychosis alone is neither necessary nor sufficient to assign a high level of concern. Its importance as a risk factor should be connected to how logically linked the symptoms are to future violence. Major depression, bipolar disorder, schizophrenia, or other psychotic disorders can all feature psychotic symptoms, which may elevate risk. Symptoms of special concern include command hallucinations, delusional beliefs of persecution or control, hostility, and grandiosity. When these symptoms co-occur with additional risk factors, particularly substance abuse or dependence, or confirmed history of violent acts and/or childhood exposure to violence, the concern may increase.

History of Suicidality

If a person of concern has threatened or attempted suicide in the past, this should trouble threat managers. Suicidal and homicidal violence are more closely linked than many realize. Evidence of suicidal thoughts is reflective of lost hope, and it may be accompanied by acceptance of the consequences for behaving violently toward others. Suicide is often contemplated by targeted violence offenders before they decide to attack; instead, they choose to punish those they feel drove them to their plight. In a study of 160 active shooter incidents in the United States between 2000 and 2013, in 64 incidents (40%), the offender committed suicide.

Weapons (firearms, edged weapons, explosives)

It is easier and more lethal to engage in targeted violence, particularly toward multiple targets, with a firearm. Possession of, access to, experience, or familiarity with weapons are all risk factors because they improve one's ability to carry out the act. Unfortunately, this can be difficult to determine in many cases. Edged weapons and stabbing instruments have been successfully used in attacks as well; they are often more accessible than firearms. Explosives: Fascination or experimentation with improvised explosive devices (IEDs) is a risk factor. They, too, increase the ability to do harm and may also indicate a study of past targeted violence incidents where IEDs were used, or their use was attempted.

Negative Family Dynamics / Support System

An unhealthy family or social peer environment can enhance risk. If there is a tacit or active endorsement of violence within the home or family sphere, this can affect how the person of concern views violence. Similarly, if law-breaking or other negative tendencies are the norms in a person's family sphere or social environment, they can influence behavior in negative ways. A toxic family or social peer dynamic could even fuel a person of concern to act. Irresponsible and chaotic families can also contribute to casual access to firearms in the home.

Isolation

Living in physical or emotional isolation from others, particularly from family and friends, deprives the person of concern of emotional support often needed to work through life's difficulties and challenges. The person has no one to rely upon. This can occur even when the person of concern shares a home with family members.

Instability
Financial, residential, professional, familial, and/or social instability all potentially interfere with the person of concern's ability to become and remain grounded and to feel emotionally safe and secure. Instability in these spheres of life can lead to grievance formation, serve as stressors, and erode coping mechanisms.

Other are Concerned
When behaviors exhibited by the person of concern cause fear in others, stakeholders should take notice. After all, individuals close to the person of concern are often best positioned to observe alarming behaviors. They may not be able to precisely articulate all of the behaviors which concern them; they just know they are troubled.

Note: Each risk factor only represents the potential for an increased likelihood of violence. No risk factor or combination of risk factors, guarantees that violence will occur or that its incidence will increase. However, the presence of these risk factors, particularly several in combination, increases the likelihood that violence will occur.

Strategies to Mitigate Risk of Violence

In addition to risk factors, warning signs, stressors, and precipitating events, safety stakeholders and threat managers should also identify the life factors present in a person of concern's life. These life factors, or threat mitigators, may prevent him/her from thinking seriously about, or completing, an act of targeted violence.

Things of Value
Persons, things, or circumstances of sufficient value to the person of concern that reduce the likelihood that he may plan and carry out an act of targeted violence

Personal Factors
Facets of the person himself which enhance his ability to cope with life's trials

External Factors
External factors which reduce the risk of planned violence, such as in relation to the target or physical environment.

The Pursuit of Non-Violent, Legally, and Socially-Sanctioned Methods of Conflict Resolution
Complaints, letters and emails, and habitual initiation of litigation are typically considered threat mitigators. These behaviors demonstrate investment in sanctioned methods of seeking redress for injustice, which therefore suggests that violence is not considered to be the only alternative. A person of concern's complaints, especially when they are constant, can be cumbersome and annoying to address; however, the devotion of energy and effort toward leveraging "the system" or communicating openly about grievances may indicate the person is more interested in venting, securing financial compensation, getting an apology, or simply being acknowledged, rather than planning future violence.

Sense of Humor
A sense of humor and the ability to laugh, in spite of life's challenges, is considered a mitigator. Laughing reduces negative physiological reactions to stress, and stress-resistant people tend to employ humor or spend time with those who do. Using humor to cope increases resilience. Review of interviews and investigative information in relation to successful and thwarted targeted violence incidents generally revealed that the offenders did not tend to use humor to cope with challenges.

Positive, Realistic Goals: Nurturing future plans and aspirations is a mitigating factor. Goals, provided they are realistic and healthy, tend to mitigate violence concerns because the person has something positive to work toward. As a more practical matter, the establishment of short- and long-term plans and goals suggests the person sees himself existing in the future, which infers the person is not considering suicide or mass homicide.

Supportive Family

At least one family member who supports intervention sets reasonable limits on behavior and provides a healthy structure, and positive influence can be a threat mitigator—the more family members who are capable and willing to fill this supportive role, the better.

Healthy Social Supports

Having a network of law-abiding friends and/or significant others around, particularly in daily life, is a mitigator. Such positive and healthy social supports act as stabilizing forces in the person's life, buffering against negative feelings, which can lead to a need to act out violently. Membership or participation in a church, law-abiding club, or community group can all qualify as mitigators. A special pet can also offer healthy support.

Positive Coping Mechanisms

A person of concern who regularly engages in positive activities such as exercise, healthy interests, or a hobby may have acquired an increased capacity to deal with stress if these are outlets unrelated to a grievance or to violence. As long as these outlets do not involve illegal, destructive, or harmful activities, they will generally be considered mitigators.

Access and Receptiveness to Assistance

Access and receptivity to needed assistance generally reduce concern because aid can often improve the quality of life in various ways. Examples include access to mental health or social services, educational or vocational assistance, outreach from family or friends, help for physical or medical conditions, financial assistance with basic needs such as food, clothing, and shelter, and any other needs the person may have.

On the Radar

The mere fact that a person of concern is the focus of an assessment and management process, with buy-in by law enforcement and safety stakeholders, is a good starting point. Active threat assessment and management allow the team to devise and implement strategies to steer the person away from violence. The effectiveness of this mitigator depends heavily on engagement by stakeholders and support from the top down in each organization involved in the process.

Note: Just as risk factors, mitigating risk factors are not to be weighted uniformly but rather individually on a case-by-case basis. A treasured relationship with one's children, for example, might have greater weight than a multitude of other mitigators or enhancers.

What We Know about Active Shooters!

Understanding the characteristics of an active shooter can give us insight into their modus operandi. The following methods are often attributed to active shooter attackers.

- The attacker is acting alone most of the time.

- The attacker may be suicidal and usually commits suicide on-site.

- The attacker almost never takes hostages nor has any interest in "negotiating."

- The attacker is preoccupied with a high body-count, which is almost always their one and only goal.

- Attackers race to murder everybody they reach in an effort to avoid contact with law enforcement.

- The majority of active shooter incidents are over within four minutes or less! Recent statistics mention the duration to be between 4 and 8 minutes. Exceptions do occur.

- The active-shooter attacker usually has multiple weapons and an ability to reload their weapons several times.

- Attackers use long arms (rifles/shotguns); almost half of the time. Handguns are the most common.
  - There is a high prediction of serious injury to the innocent and unarmed!

- Active shooter attackers may be stopped by non-police, armed security personnel, police intervention, or by themselves - committing suicide.

* modus operandi (noun) a particular way or method of doing something, especially one that is characteristic or well-established.

Chapter 4

Vigilance for Violence

Vigilance is the <u>practice</u> of paying attention to our internal and external messages with regard to ourselves, other people, things, and events. Vigilance is our internal and external safe- guard against an Active Shooter situation. We sometimes feel something isn't right (internal) and sometimes see that some- thing isn't right (external).

"Eternal vigilance is the price of liberty."

- Thomas Jefferson

Have you ever had a pause about a person, place, thing, or event?

- Our intuitive ability is a component of our vigilance.

When we are Vigilant, we are:

- Watchful and Alert
- Observant and Attentive
- Present to what is happening and what can happen

NOTE: Hypervigilance is a negative condition of maintaining an abnormal awareness of environmental stimuli that causes anxiety, leads to exhaustion, and causes us to startle easily. Hypervigilance is counter-productive and unhealthy. Learning the AVADE® principles will give you the tools you need to live a happy, safe life without allowing fear to consume you.

The five senses warn us of danger and keep us safe: touch, smell, hearing, taste, and sight, are the ways our minds and bodies connect to the outer world. Our senses can also alert us and keep us safe from danger. Many people believe that there is a sixth sense.

Is there a Sixth Sense?

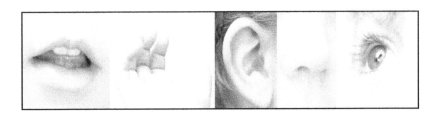

Do you know the sound of a gunshot?

Would you deny that you heard a gunshot?

What are some noises that may sound like a gunshot?
- Firecracker
- Car Backfiring
- Someone dropping something (loud noise)

We may deny what we hear or see. Denial is our enemy and steals our time!

Time and distance from an Active Shooter can ultimately keep us safe.

Don't let denial rob you of precious time!

Trust Your Intuition, your sixth sense.
Intuition is knowing without knowing why. Intuition communicates with us through symbols, feelings, and emotions. It's like a radar for sensing, seeing, or feeling danger before it is present.

Intuition is a personal security system that is always on and ever vigilant, surveying not only danger, but everything else as well.

Trust your intuition!
Intuition is a process of gaining information that does not rely on your senses, memory, experiences, or thought processes. However, it uses this information to help interpret the information gained.

"The intuitive mind is a sacred gift, and the rational mind is a faithful servant. We have created a society that honors the servant and has forgotten the gift." - Albert Einstein

Using Your Intuition

The ability to read a person's attitudes and thoughts by their behaviors was the original communication system used by humans prior to spoken language. In his book *Body Talk*: *The Meaning of Human Gestures*, author Desmond Morris lists more than fifty body signals (messages) that are universal to all human beings in every culture. The majority of these messages are communicated unconsciously. Just as the communication is unconscious, so is our ability to read this nonverbal communication. If you were asked to identify just ten of these nonverbal messages, you might find it difficult, but we all know them and respond to them intuitively. The key to using your intuition more effectively is to bring the unconscious data it supplies to a place where your conscious mind can interpret it. Intuition is always communicating with you. Occasionally it may send a signal about something that turns out to be less than dangerous, but everything it communicates to you is meaningful.

Intuition might send any of several messengers to get your attention, and because they differ according to urgency, it is good to know the various messages.

Messages of Intuition

- **Synchronicity**
  This is a message all of us get. It's the connectedness we all have and write off as airy-fairy. The best example of this is a phone call. All of us have been thinking about that particular someone, and the phone rings, and it's them. This happens to all of us in many ways every day.

- **Nagging Feelings**
  When we experience nagging feelings about someone or something, it is our unconscious awareness telling us to wait and question what is going on.

- **Hunches**
  A hunch is a feeling that a particular event or situation will go a certain way.

- **Gut Feeling**
  A term many of us like to use in regard to predicting something that may or may not happen. For some of us, a gut feeling is visceral- we can literally feel it.

- **Hesitation/Doubt**
  When we hesitate or find ourselves having doubts, we are stalling for more time and questioning the situation.

- **Suspicion**
  For some, being suspicious is their internal radar telling them, "something isn't right here." Even the Federal Government encourages this message of intuition in its campaign "if you see something, say something."
  - *Report Suspicious Activity to local authorities.*
  - To report suspicious activity, contact your local law en-forcement agency.
  - Describe specifically what you observed, including:

Who or what you saw;

When you saw it;

Where it occurred; and

Why it's suspicious.

If there is an emergency, call 9–1–1

- **Physical Changes**
  Like other species, we too change physically when exposed to internal and external intuitive messages. When the hair stands up on the back of your neck or when you get goose bumps, your body is telling you something.

- **Sense of Danger:** The intuitive messenger with the greatest urgency is **DANGER**. When you know with all of your being that you are in trouble or a situation is imminent, this is the intuitive message of danger.

Developing Intuition

Learning to read body language teaches us to be more sensi-tive to people's feelings and emotions, provide better customer service or care to those who rely on us and increase our per-sonal safety. Developing your intuitive ability begins with paying attention to what's going on inside of you so that you can become aware of these inner signals and catch them when they are happening or shortly afterward.

NOTE: Besides denial, another enemy of intuition is worry. When you mentally or replay in your mind negative situations, spending energy on things that have already happened or might happen soon, you don't have the mental space to acknowledge and act on signals your intuition is trying to send to you!

Stop-Look-Listen

Developing and using your intuition means you need to stop, look, and occasionally listen to what your feelings, senses, perceptions, and the contexts of situations are telling you at that present moment. Listening to, trusting, and acting on your intuitive inner guidance is an art. And like any art or discipline, it requires an ongoing commitment. Challenge yourself to develop a deeper understanding of self-awareness.

Chapter 5

Who Commits Violence?

Answer: People do! The types of individuals who commit violence are categorized into five areas: stranger violence, guest/client violence, lateral violence, domestic violence, and extreme violence.

Stranger	Patient/Client	Lateral	Domestic	Extreme

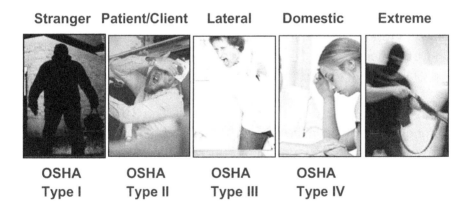

OSHA	OSHA	OSHA	OSHA	
Type I	Type II	Type III	Type IV	

There are specific characteristics for all five types of individual violence listed above. The AVADE® Training program for workplace violence prevention thoroughly examines these characteristics and provides strategies to prevent, mitigate and eliminate your risk of violence from these individuals. For the purposes of this book on Active Shooters, we will identify the characteristics of the violent individual who could precipitate an Active Shooter incident.

Of these five types of individuals who commit violence, which ones could be an Active Shooter? – All of them could! We often categorize stranger and extreme violence as our Active Shooters, but any of them could be and have been an Active Shooter.

Stranger Violence = Active Shooter
On November 27, 2015, a gunman attacked a Planned Parenthood clinic in Colorado Springs, Colorado. A police officer and two civilians were killed; five police officers and four civilians were injured. After a standoff that lasted five hours, police SWAT teams crashed armored vehicles into the lobby, and the attacker surrendered.

Client/Patient Violence = Active Shooter
On April 19, 2010, a gunman armed with a handgun began shooting in Parkwest Medical Center in Knoxville, TN. The man shot and killed a woman, wounded two others, and then killed himself. He believed a doctor had implanted a tracking chip in his body during an appendectomy.

Lateral Violence = Active Shooter
On December 2, 2015, 14 people were killed, and 22 were seri- ously injured in a terrorist attack (lateral violence) at the Inland Regional Center in San Bernardino, California, which con- sisted of a mass shooting and an attempted bombing. The perpetrators, a married couple living in the city of Redlands, targeted a San Bernardino County Department of Public Health training event and Christmas party, of about 80 employees, in a rented banquet room. The male shooter worked for the county as a health department employee. After the shooting, the couple fled in a rented sport utility vehicle (SUV). Four hours later, police pursued their vehicle and killed them in a shootout.

Domestic Violence = Active Shooter
An Active Shooter incident occurred on October 12, 2011, at the Salon Meritage hair salon in Seal Beach, California. Eight people inside the salon and one person in the parking lot were shot, and

only one victim survived. The shooter was involved in a custody dispute (domestic violence) with his ex-wife, whom he later shot and killed. The shooter was armed with three handguns and reloaded at least once during the attack, which lasted two minutes. There were about twenty people in the sa- lon at the time; some managed to escape by running into the street or hiding in neighboring businesses. Six people were declared dead at the scene, and three survivors were taken to a hospital, where two of them later died of their wounds.

Extreme Violence = Active Shooter
On November 5, 2009, a mass shooting took place at Fort Hood Army base near Killeen, Texas. A U.S. Army major and psychiatrist fatally shot 13 people and injured more than 30 others. Many have called the event a terrorist attack (extreme violence). The United States Department of Defense and federal law enforcement agencies had classified the shootings as an act of workplace violence.

Don't Be Easy Prey:
Don't Be a Victim of Violence!

Any of the mental states or what are known as Victim Paradigms listed below leave you vulnerable to violence. Do not fall into these mental states— that's one of your best defenses for avoiding violence.

Un-Aware Unconsciously: An unconscious state of unawareness of a person's surroundings and the people they encounter. This unconscious state is not knowing that you don't know. But remember, ignorance is not a good defense.

Un-Prepared: A higher state of conscious awareness than be- ing un-aware, but lacking in preparedness for potential situations. Have you ever said to yourself, "I'm just not that pre- pared for the day"?

Un-Secured: Not making good use of the precautionary security tools and equipment in a person's environment. Environmental components are in place to keep you safe. Not knowing where they are or how to use them is not a good defense.

Un-Aware Consciously: The most lacking in awareness is a dangerous state of denial—the "nothing can happen to me" mentality. It's when you just don't care and are consciously choosing to be unaware

Un-Fortunate: Being in the wrong place at the wrong time. This paradigm mindset is the least likely to happen; however, by in- creasing your awareness and your vigilance, you can lessen your chances of being in the wrong place at the wrong time.

Active Shooter Characteristics

When you have an understanding of the characteristics of individuals who commit violence, it can increase your awareness and vigilance. This is the antidote to victim paradigms.

Active Shooters are motivated by:

EVIL: The active shooter may be profoundly immoral and wicked, especially when motivated or inspired by a supernatural force.

Anger: The active shooter may have a perception of having been offended or wronged and a tendency to undo that wrongdoing by retaliation.

Justice: In its broadest sense, the active shooter believes that people receive that which they deserve based on their interpretation of what constitutes fairness.

Desire: The active shooter may have a desire for notoriety or recognition. The desire could be to solve a problem that is perceived to be unbearable—the desire to kill or be killed.

Ideology: The active shooter may be motivated by extremist views, including religious, political, racist, and single-issue ideologies.

Religion: Religious violence is violence that is motivated by, or in reaction to, religious precepts, texts, or the doctrines of a target or an attacker. It includes violence against religious institutions, people, objects, or events

Revenge: The active shooter may be seeking revenge for a perceived injury or grievance.

Notoriety: Some active shooters are motivated by a desire for fame, notoriety, and/or recognition

Retaliation: The action of counter-attacking is based on a perception that the individual was harmed.

Mental Illness: Severe mental illness, particularly psychosis, co-occurring with additional risk factors, particularly substance abuse or dependence, or confirmed history of violent acts and/or childhood exposure to violence may motivate the active shooter.

Media Stardom: When the media focuses on the shooter, they provide this fame, notoriety, and recognition.

Predictions of Violence

It may be difficult to predict that an individual will commit an act of violence, but not impossible. There are signs and symptoms that a person is escalating into violence. Many offenders who engage in targeted violence may display certain behaviors during preattack planning. The list below summarizes some which may indicate increasing concern. This list is not necessarily exhaustive, and other behaviors of concern may be evident. These behaviors may be observable to persons familiar with the person of concern, and assessors should bear these in mind during encounters with him. No one behavior, standing alone, should be considered conclusive to a violence concern; rather, all behaviors and circumstances should always be considered in totality.

Recognizing early warning signs of Violence

A single early warning sign may not be a red flag (or it may), but a combination of any of the following signs should be cause for concern and action. Always report what you see and hear!

- **Direct or Verbal Threats of Harm.**
    - o   Intimidation of others by words and/or actions.
    - o   Repeatedly verbalizing that something will happen to someone against whom the individual has a grudge.

- **Sudden change in social media behavior.**
    - o   Including but not necessarily limited to the use of encryption, decrease in postings, increase in postings, leakage, or novel use of different platforms.

- **The recent acquisition of weapons.**
    - o   Ammunition, personal protective gear, tactical clothing, or other items which is a departure from the individual's normal patterns.

- o The recent escalation in target practice and weapons training may also be a concern if he previously owned weapons and ammunition.

- **Recent interest in explosive devices or acquisition of parts to construct one.**

- **Signs of research, planning, and preparation which are contextually inappropriate in the person of concern's everyday life.**

- **Contextually inappropriate, intense interest in or fascination with previous shooting incidents or mass assaults.**
  - o This may include identification with perpetrators of violence, particularly mass violence, and such identifications may be with either fictional or nonfictional persons.

- **History of stalking, harassing, threatening, or menacing behavior.**

- **Increased use of alcohol and/or illegal drugs.**
  - o Sudden cessation of medications or other substance use.

- **Depression/withdrawal and/or expression of extreme desperation over recent problems.**
  - o Others are concerned

- **Noticeable decrease in attention to appearance and hygiene.**
  - o Drastic changes in appearance such as a shaved head, large or multiple tattoos, contextually inappropriate law enforcement or military costuming, sudden weight loss or gain, cessation of hygiene, or sudden unkempt appearance.

- **Resistance and overreaction to changes in policy and procedures.**
  - Repeated violations of company policies or refusing to follow policies.
  - History of non-compliance with limits and boundaries (work/personal).

- **Increasing in number or severity of mood swings.**
  - Noticeably unstable emotional responses.
  - Explosive outbursts of anger or rage without provocation.

- **Suicidal; statements or behaviors which seem to indicate suicidality.**
  - End-of-life planning
  - Interest in destructiveness toward the world at large.
  - Preparation of "statement" or farewell writings, to include manifestos, videos, notes, internet blogs, or emails.
  - Last resort warning behavior.

- **Paranoia or paranoid behavior ("everybody is against me").**
  - Hypersensitivity/extreme suspiciousness.

- **Increasingly talks of problems at home.**
  - An escalation of domestic problems in the workplace.
  - Negative family dynamics and support system.
  - Talk of severe financial problems.

- **Recent and significant personal loss or humiliation, whether real or simply perceived, such as a death, breakup or divorce, or loss of a job, status, or self-image.**

- **Extreme moral righteousness**
  - Inability to take criticism regarding job performance.
  - Holding a grudge, especially against a supervisor.

- **Intentional disregard for the safety of others, including the destruction of property.**

- o Recent acts of novel or experimental aggression, including trespass, animal cruelty, or vandalism.

- **Sudden withdrawal from a normal life pattern.**
  - o Retreating to temporary quarters, absence from work without explanation.
  - o Failing to appear for appointments that are normally kept.
  - o Isolation and Instability.
  - o Unexplained increase in absenteeism; vague physical complaints.
  - o Sudden onset of reckless sexual, financial, or other behaviors that may suggest a lack of concern for future consequences.

- **Any effort to physically approach an apparent target or close associates, evidence of items left for the target to find even if they appear benign (such as flowers), evidence of surveillance without approach, or attempts to breach or circumvent security measures.**

- **Direct or indirect communications or threats using multiple methods of delivery, such as email, facsimile, hand-delivery, text message, etc., escalating in frequency or intensity, or which demonstrate that actual surveillance has occurred.**

An assailant who commits a threat or assault may be seeking revenge for perceived unfair treatment. **Any workplace can be at risk of violence**.

Pre-Incident Reporting: Signs of violence should be reported via your incident reporting procedures.

The 5 Stages of an Active Shooter:

- **Fantasy Stage**
- **Planning Stage**
- **Preparation Stage**
- **Approach Stage**
- **Implementation Stage**

Fantasy stage: Initially, the shooter only dreams of the shooting. He fantasizes about the headlines and the news coverage he'll receive. He pictures breaking the death count record of the previous active shooter and going out in a blaze of glory. He may draw pictures of the event, post them on the web, and even discuss these desires with friends and foes alike. If these fantasies are passed on to law enforcement, police intervention can take place prior to the suspect's attack. In this case, there may even be zero casualties.

Planning stage: The suspect is still a potential active shooter at this stage. He is determining logistics – the who, what, when, where, and how of the infamous day. He may put plans down in writing and will often discuss these plans with others. A time and location will be decided upon – one that will ensure the greatest number of victims or, in some cases, target specific individuals. The potential shooter will determine the weapons needed and how they will be obtained. He will decide how to travel to the target location and how to dress to conceal his weapons without arousing suspicion. If the police are tipped off at this time, intervention may be made with zero casualties.

Preparation stage: A law enforcement agency can still intervene during the preparation stage. The suspect may be obtaining gun powder or other chemicals for his improvised explosive devices. He might break into a house to steal weapons and ammunition and/or hide them away in a designated place closer to where he plans to attack. He may also do a practice run or walkthrough of the operation, gearing himself up for the assault. Potential shooters have been known to call friends and tell them not to go to school or work on a certain day in order to keep them out of the line of fire. If one of these people informs the police of their concerns, there is another opportunity for law enforcement to intervene before the event. If this is the case, there is a real possibility that there may be zero casualties.

Approach stage: The closer the time to the planned event, the more dangerous it will be for an officer to take action. By the approach stage, the suspect has made his plans and has committed himself to carrying out the act. At this point, he is actually moving toward the intended target and will most likely be carrying the tools that he'll use for the massacre. Officers may come into contact with the suspect at this stage because of a citizen complaint, a traffic stop, or something similar. A thorough investigation can lead to an arrest of the suspect before he brings down a multitude of innocent people in a shooting or bombing. However dangerous, the stop-an alert and armed officer has a final chance to intervene. The officer must be prepared and aware during every street contact. This contact could become a lifesaver and may end in zero casualties.

The Implementation stage: Once the shooter opens fire, immediate action must be taken. Initial responding officers need to immediately proceed to the suspect and stop the threat. If he is not stopped, the active shooter will continue to kill until he runs out of victims or ammunition. Remember, the active shooter is unique because he is going for the "top score" or the highest number of kills on record for an active shooter incident. It is almost like a bizarre video game, except it's real.

https://www.policeone.com/active-shooter/articles/5844457-Colo-massacre-Educating-the-public-on-the-five-phases-of-the-active-shooter/

Chapter 6

YOU Have the Right to Defend Yourself

"The best self-defense is to not be there when the attack takes place."- David Fowler, author of
Be Safe Not Sorry and Violence in the Workplace

Self-defense is the right to use **reasonable force** to protect one's self or members of one's staff/family from bodily harm from the attack of an aggressor, if you have reason to believe that you or they are in danger. Self-defense must always be your last resort. When it is used, the force used must be considered "reasonable,"; e.g., striking someone who yells an obscenity at you is not considered "reasonable force."

The best self-defense is to avoid the situation and get away. If avoidance and escape are not possible, a reasonable defense would be lawful as a last resort. You have the right to defend yourself; however, any use of self-defense must follow any agency policy and procedure, as well as comply with state and federal law.

The following information will provide a general understanding of what self-defense and use-of-force are and how you can legally protect yourself against assault and liability risk associated with any type of self-defense or force.

Disclaimer

This chapter will give you a basic understanding of self-defense, assault, reasonable force, and basic legal definitions of force. Personal Safety Training Inc. makes no legal declaration, rep- resentation, or claim as to what force should be used or not used during a self-defense or assault incident or situation. Each individual must take into consideration their ability, agency policies and procedures, and laws in the state and country in which they reside.

Types of Assault

Physical Assault: The attempt to cause injury, coupled with the present ability to cause injury.

Non-Physical Assault: Physical contact is not required to constitute an assault. In all states, threats are a separate crime. A verbal threat of physical harm is a threat with the intent to intimidate or scare, resulting in the alteration of any part of a person's normal life due to the threat.

To constitute an illegal threat, the following must be true:
- The threat must be serious, with the threat of definite injury
- The threat must be immediate and can be carried out in the immediate or near future.
- The threat must be credible; that is, the victim believes the threat and acts upon that belief.

Domestic Assault: Can involve battery that occurs between two parties who are related to some degree (family or intimate relationships).

Battery Assault: Battery is a criminal offense whereby one party makes physical contact with another party with the intention to harm them. In order to constitute a battery, an offense must be intentional and must be committed to inflicting injury on another.

Sexual Battery: Any non-consensual physical contact that is sexual in nature.

Lawful Use of Defense
In order to be lawful in your defense of yourself and others, you must have a basic understanding of some legal definitions and how they apply to self-defense and our legal system.

1. Use-of-Force
2. Reasonable Force
3. Reasonable Belief
4. Deadly Force
5. Excessive Force
6. Dangerous & Deadly Weapons

Use-of-Force

A term that describes the right of an individual or authority to settle conflicts or prevent certain actions by applying measures to either:
- Dissuade another party from a particular course of action,…or
- Physically intervene to stop or control them.

Reasonable Force: The degree of force which is not excessive and is appropriate in protecting one's self or one's property.
- When such force is used, a person is justified and is not criminally liable, nor liable in tort. (A tort is an act that damages someone in some way and for which the injured person may sue the wrongdoer for damages.)

Reasonable Belief: The facts or circumstances that an individual knows, or should know, are such as to cause an ordinary and prudent person to act or think in a similar way under similar circumstances.

Deadly Force: Force that is likely or intended to cause death or great bodily harm. Deadly force may be reasonable or unreasonable, depending on the circumstances.

Excessive Force: That amount of force which is beyond the need and circumstances of the particular event, or which is not justified in the light of all the circumstances, for instance, in the case of deadly force to protect property as contrasted with protecting life.

Dangerous and Deadly Weapons

"Dangerous Weapon" is a device or in-strument which, in the manner it is used, or intended to be used, is calculated or likely to produce death or great bodily harm.

"Deadly Weapons" includes any firearm, whether loaded or unloaded, or a device designed as a weapon and capable of producing death or great bodily harm.

Levels of Force and Defense

The following chart is designed to give you a basic understanding of how your actions may apply to the actions of an aggressive subject. You may need to increase or decrease your action level, depending on the situation. Any Use-of-Force or Self-Defense MUST be lawful.

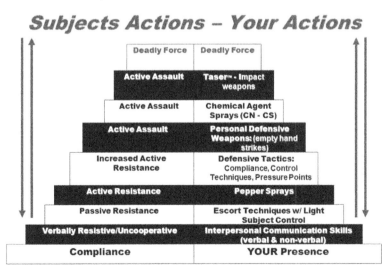

Subjects Actions – Your Actions

Deadly Force	Deadly Force
Active Assault	Taser™ - Impact weapons
Active Assault	Chemical Agent Sprays (CN - CS)
Active Assault	Personal Defensive Weapons: (empty hand strikes)
Increased Active Resistance	Defensive Tactics: Compliance, Control Techniques, Pressure Points
Active Resistance	Pepper Sprays
Passive Resistance	Escort Techniques w/ Light Subject Control
Verbally Resistive/Uncooperative	Interpersonal Communication Skills (verbal & non-verbal)
Compliance	YOUR Presence

Lawful Use-of-Force & Defense is permissible:

1. When used to control an out-of-control individual
2. When used to overcome the resistance of the out-of-control individual
3. When used to prevent escape from an individual who is under your control (hold)
4. When used in self-defense or in defense of others

Use-of-Force & Self-Defense MUST be Reasonable

YOU should always take into consideration the facts and the circumstances of the incident.

- Type of crime and severity of the crime

- The resistance of the subject when needing to control them

- The threat and safety to others in the area

- Aggressive Subject and Staff Factors

Aggressive Subject and Staff Factors

Many factors may affect your selection of an appropriate level of use-of-force or self-defense. These factors should be articulated in your post-incident documentation.

Examples may include:

Age: In dealing with an aggressive subject who is agile, younger, faster, stronger, and has more stamina, an older staff person may have to use more force/control/defense. In contrast, a younger staff person might need to use less control/force/defense on an older person.

Size: In dealing with a larger aggressive subject, a smaller staff person may need to use more force/control/defense during the incident. A larger staff person would obviously use less force/control/defense with an aggressive subject who is smaller.

Skill Level: In dealing with a subject skilled in mixed martial arts or an expert in karate, it may be more difficult to control or defend against them based on their skill level. A staff person who is skilled in defensive tactics may only need to use a minimum of force (with proper technique) to control/defend the subject. A staff person without current training and experience may need to use more force/defense to control or defend against the subject.

Relative Strength: The different body composition of males and females may be a factor in controlling a member of the opposite gender. Females typically have less torso strength than their male counterparts. Male staff may need less force to control a female subject, while a female staff person may need to use more force to control a male subject.

Multiple Aggressors: A staff person who is being physically attacked by multiple aggressors is at a disadvantage. Even highly skilled staff member involved in defensive tactics is likely to be harmed in a situation such as this. In order to survive multiple aggressor attacks, higher levels of force may be necessary.

Special Note:
Every person must take into consideration their moral, legal, and ethical beliefs, rights, and understandings when using any type of force to defend themselves or others. Personal Safety Training Inc. makes no legal declaration, representation, or claim as to what force should be used or not used during a self-defense/assault incident or situation. Each individual must take into consideration their ability, agency policies and procedures, and laws in their state and/or country.

Chapter 7

The Stress Continuum

The Stress Continuum

- **Stress** is physical, emotional, or mental strain or tension brought on by internal and external factors.

- **Fear** is a distressing emotion aroused by a perceived threat. It is a basic survival mechanism that occurs in response to a specific stimulus, such as pain or the threat of danger.

- **Fight-Flight-Freeze** is a reaction to a threat with a general discharge of the sympathetic nervous system, priming the organism for fighting or fleeing.

Stress + Fear = Fight-Flight-Freeze

You may wonder why this is even being discussed?

Won't an active shooter situation be incredibly stressful? Yes, it will! And we need to understand that the stress continuum, if not broken, can leave us with a primal response, which could lead us to freeze. And the last thing we want to do in an active shooter situation is FREEZE! The following information will help us understand the stress continuum and, ultimately, how to break it.

Fear

Some psychologists suggest that fear belongs to a small set of basic or innate emotions. This set also includes such emotions as joy, sadness, and anger. Fear should be distinguished from the related emotional state of anxiety, which typically occurs without any external threat.

Fear may be induced whether the threat is real or imagined.

Additionally, fear is related to the specific behaviors of escape and avoidance, whereas stress is the result of threats that are perceived to be uncontrollable or unavoidable. Worth noting is that fear almost always relates to future events, such as worsening of a situation or continuation of a situation that is unacceptable. Fear could also be an instant reaction to something currently happening.

"Fight-Flight-Freeze"

You've heard of fight-or-flight, which is a reaction to a threat with a general discharge of the sympathetic nervous system, priming the organism for fighting or fleeing. But, Freeze?

If completely overwhelmed, a person may freeze.

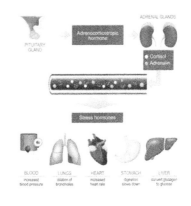

The **fight-flight-freeze response** is a basic, primal, physiological urge to defend or to flee in times of danger. When faced with a situation that is frightening, your perception of it stimulates the part of the brain called the hypothalamus. The hypothalamus emits a hormone that stimulates the pituitary gland to release substances that excite the adrenal gland to release adrenalin (epinephrine) and cortisone.

- Adrenalin stimulates the heart to beat faster and the vessels carrying blood to the muscles to open.

- The vessels that run the digestive and eliminative organs constrict. Blood pressure goes up, and more blood is being pumped, but many vessels constrict to slow the blood flow.
- Breath becomes faster and shallower, or you hold your breath.
- Blood shunts systematically from the vegetative organs to the muscles preparing you to fight or take flight.

Putting the Brakes on the Fight-Flight-Freeze (Stress Continuum)

Awareness Controlled Breathing and **Awareness Positive Thinking** are considered the best stress management techniques for immediate stressors (fight-flight) and for the ongoing stressors of life.

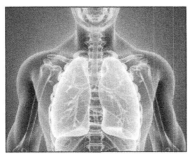

Awareness Controlled Breathing is a very useful tactic in lowering our blood pressure. Studies have shown that during the process of slow, deep breathing, endorphins are released, causing a feeling of general well-being and relaxation. Endorphins apply a brake to the hypothalamic fight-flight response in a situation of imminent danger. Try this: inhale slowly, about two-thirds of your lung capacity. Breathe in for a count of four seconds; breathe out slowly to a count of eight seconds. Notice you immediately feel calmer.

Awareness Positive Thinking, and calm mental preparation were recognized to be highly valuable to the Samurai of feudal Japan. In fact, the Samurai spent as much time in mental training as they did preparing their bodies for battle. Samurai employed two techniques to prepare 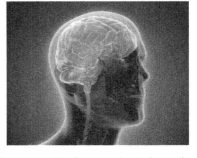 the mind to be tranquil, fearless, and energetic in combat: breath control and meditation. The Samurai knew that a warrior filled with fear (negative thoughts) was doomed. Fear inhibits the ability to think quickly or to act fully.

Any type of violence can be devastating to deal with. If you have suffered from a violent incident, you may need to seek some type of assistance, e.g., (Employee Assistance Program).

Learning and integrating the AVADE® techniques in this training course and in all of the AVADE® training programs will help ensure that you know what to do in a violent encounter. This will reduce the chances of YOU becoming a victim of violence.

Post-Incident Stress Debriefing for Violence

The methods described above help manage your stress before an incident occurs. The methods described below will help you manage stress after an incident of workplace violence.

- **Always debrief.** Staff should debrief after every workplace violence incident, regardless of the severity. Oftentimes a brief discussion of the events and outcome is enough. Other times, a more intensive debriefing is needed.
  - **The goal of debriefing is to reduce the chances of Post-Traumatic Stress Symptoms and Post Traumatic Stress Disorder (PTSD).**

- **Acknowledge humanness.** As humans, we are susceptible to the frailties of human nature. This acknowledgement creates an awareness that it is okay to seek and ask for help.

- **Talk to co-workers.** Almost all workers have experienced or witnessed some type of workplace violence incident. Your co-workers can be a great resource to vent your concerns about your feelings after an incident.

- Be aware of post-event feelings. Having the knowledge and

awareness that you may experience strong feelings from an event can give you the confidence to seek help and discuss feelings with others.

- **Take advantage of your Employee Assistance Program (EAP).** Agencies realize that feelings may persist for longer than you might expect after an incident. Employee Assistance Programs can benefit employees and help them deal with post-incident stress or other work/personal problems. EAPs are intended to help employees deal with problems or issues that might adversely affect their work performance, health, and well-being. EAPs generally include assessment, short-term counseling, and referral services for employees and their household members.

- **Know the signs and symptoms of Post-Traumatic Stress Disorder (PTSD).** PTSD is a psychological reaction occurring after experiencing a highly stressful event (such as wartime combat, physical violence, or a natural disaster). It's usually characterized by depression, anxiety, flashbacks, recurrent nightmares, and avoidance of reminders of the event.

- **Take the time to follow up with other staff.** As human beings, we often focus on the needs of others and not ourselves. Take the time to discuss workplace incidents, your feelings about the incidents, and how dealing with incidents in the workplace could improve.

Critical Incident Stress Debriefing (CISD)

- Debriefing is a specific technique designed to assist people in dealing with the physical or psychological symptoms that are generally associated with trauma exposure.

- Debriefing allows those involved with the incident to process the event and reflect on its impact.

Individuals who are exposed to an assault situation (as a witness or a victim) should consider some level of critical incident debriefing or counseling.

The final extent of any traumatic situation may never be known or realistically estimated in terms of trauma, loss, and grief. In the aftermath of any critical incident, psychological reactions are quite common and are fairly predictable. CISD can be a valuable tool following a traumatic event.

Research on the effectiveness of critical incident debriefing techniques has demonstrated that individuals who are provided CISD within a 24- to 72-hour period after the critical incident experience lower levels of short- and long-term crisis reactions, psychological trauma, and PTSD.

Conducting an Incident Debrief

Staff should debrief after every workplace violence incident, regardless of the severity. Oftentimes a brief discussion of the events and outcome is enough. Other times, a more intensive debriefing is needed. **Debriefs are always POSITIVE!**
After action, corrections should be done at a later date.
There are four primary steps for conducting an Incident Debrief:
1. **Wellness Check:** the facilitator conducting the debrief asks each person involved and gets a verbal acknowledgement of their mental and physical wellness.
2. **What Happened:** the facilitator conducting the debrief asks each person to briefly describe what they saw, heard, and experienced during the incident.
3. **What did WE do well:** the facilitator conducting the debrief will ask each person to briefly describe what the team (we) did well in responding to and dealing with the incident.
4. **What can WE Improve Upon:** the facilitator conducting the debrief will ask each person to briefly describe what they believe the team (we) can improve upon in future incidents. Positive!!

| | AVADE°DEBRIEF PROCESS FORM |

▶ Conducting an Incident Debrief

- ☑ After a violent incident, it is important that **all personnel involved in the incident meet immediately following the incident to debrief.**

- ☑ The debrief should be **led and documented by the supervisor and/or person in charge on duty** at the time of the incident, in coordination with security personnel.

FOUR PRIMARY STEPS TO CONDUCTING AN INCIDENT DEBRIEF:

1. **Wellness Check:** The facilitator conducting the debrief *asks each person* involved and gets a *verbal acknowledgement* of their **mental** and **physical wellness.**
   - The debrief leader will **assist in determining if anyone requires immediate or follow up medical treatment** as a result of *injury sustained* as a *result of the incident.*
   - If any personnel are identified as *sustaining injury* or *experiencing extensive stress* as a result of the incident, the agency will need to **follow up and provide further support and resources,** in line with the facilities policy & procedures.

2. **What Happened:** The facilitator conducting the debrief *ask each person* to briefly **describe what they saw, heard and experienced** during the incident.
   - It is important to assist in creating an environment within the debrief that allows **ALL individuals involved** to appropriately decompress and gain their composure prior to returning to regular job duties.

3. **What Did We Do Well:** The facilitator conducting the debrief will *ask each person* to briefly **describe what the team (we) did well** in responding and dealing with the incident?
   - Often, individuals *immediately following an event* will still be experiencing a **high level of adrenaline.** This is especially true for those who may have not experienced a violent event very often.

4. **What Can we Improve Upon:** The facilitator conducting the debrief will ask each person to briefly describe what they believe the team (we) can improve upon in future incidents? Positive!!
   - An individual still experiencing an *adrenaline rush,* may not be aware of their need to decompress or how the incident may have impacted them emotionally and/or mentally. Because of this, as a **TEAM,** ensure that you encourage each other to take a moment and *assess your ability to return to your regular job duties.*

Staff should debrief after every workplace violence incident, *regardless of the severity.* Often times a brief discussion of the events and outcome is enough. Other times, a more intensive debriefing is needed. Debriefs are **always POSITIVE!** After action corrections should be *done at a later date.*

Remember: The goal of debriefing is to **reduce the chances of Post-Traumatic Stress Disorder** (PTSD) and **Post-Traumatic Stress Symptoms.**

A) Wellness Check: _____

_____

B) What Happened: _____

_____

C) What Did We Do Well: _____

_____

D) What Can We Improve Upon: _____

_____

Education, Prevention, and Mitigation for *Violence in the Workplace*

© Personal Safety Training Inc. | AVADE® Training

Chapter 8

Escape-Escape-Escape

Escape Planning

Developing escape plans for your various environments prepares you for the unfortunate event that you may need to escape from an Active Shooter or dangerous situation. This preparation is not intended to make you scared or paranoid but to prepare you for the unexpected.

"Prepare for the worst, hope for the best, and expect some surprises along the way." - David Fowler, author, and creator of AVADE® Training

The first thing is to learn where all the exits are, wherever you are, in any environment. It's a habit that could save your life. But not only are physical escapes needed, but so are quick verbal responses that detach you from potential situations that can be negative, threatening, and potentially dangerous or embarrassing.

Rules for Surviving an Active Shooter

1. **Escape (RUN) if safe to do so!**
2. HIDE and cover in place if you cannot escape. (SAFE ROOM)
3. Alert (911) authorities—police, armed security.
4. Lock doors in your immediate area.
5. Place barriers and remain absolutely quiet.
6. If escape is not possible and danger is imminent, (FIGHT) attack the attacker.
7. When law enforcement arrives, be submissive, expose your palms, and do what they tell you to do.

In this chapter, we will focus on Rule #1 – Escape if safe to do so!

Imagine, right now, that you hear gunshots outside the room you are in.

- Are you able to escape?
- Is there only one escape route? If so, is that where the gunshots are coming from?
- Is there an alternate escape route in your environment?
- Are there others in the room who would not be able to escape with you?
- Are you willing to leave them if they are unwilling or unable to leave the area?
- Are you prepared mentally to deal with this situation?

These are questions that you must be willing to answer if you want to be prepared for an active shooter situation. Trying to determine what our responses would be once the gunshots begin usually leads to becoming overwhelmed by the stress and fear and freezing.

Escape (RUN) if safe to do so!

- **Have an escape route & plan in mind**
  Make a commitment to know your escape route in all of the environments you are in. This takes practice and commitment. Your continual commitment will create a habit, and personal safety habits are an unconscious awareness that will keep you safe.

- **Leave your personal belongings behind**
  Is there any personal belonging you have that is worth your life? No!!! Not your phone, your car keys, pictures, laptop, or anything else. Leave it and get out if you can.

- **Help others escape, if possible**
  Obviously, we will help our family members (children) escape from a violent situation. But… what if I am at work and my co-workers refuse to leave. Leave them! Encourage them to leave; you can't force them.

- **Evacuate regardless of others (HEALTHCARE SITUATIONS)**
  What if… I work in a hospital, and I have patients that I am caring for? Do I leave them? Yes and No – let's start with the no. In certain circumstances/environments where you do not leave your patients because they are unable (non-ambulatory), you may end up injured, shot, and/or killed. An individual MUST decide for him or herself if they are willing to stay with their non-moveable patients/clients. If you do leave them, it is not abandonment; it is your safety! This is a huge dilemma in social services and healthcare where you may not be able to evacuate with your patients/clients. Your option may be Rule #2 (HIDE and Cover in Place). Again, when the shots are fired, it's often too late to decide what to do. Decide now! Have a plan and a backup plan.

- **Warn/prevent individuals from entering**
  "There's a shooter in the building; don't go in!" Warning people of imminent danger so that they do not walk into the violence is absolutely encouraged. Wouldn't you want to know what was going on inside the area you were about to enter.? Some people may not believe you or care and proceed in. But at least you have warned them and done your part.

- **Do not attempt to move wounded people**
  Trying to move a wounded person is a compassionate and caring thing to do. However, it could expose you to being shot and injured or killed. The police and paramedics will move and take care of anyone who is left in the area that cannot move on their own. This may not be immediate, and we must accept this reality. Remember, your plan is to ESCAPE!

To expedite your escape, there are certain levels of awareness that you may find valuable. Let's refresh our understanding of these: Environmental Awareness and 360-Degree Environmental Awareness.

Environmental Awareness
Environmental awareness is the ability to understand and recognize the many factors relating to your environment and how they can benefit you or limit you.

It also means having: **An understanding that your external physical conditions can affect and influence your growth, development, and physical survival.**

Creating an awareness of what is around you at all times is described as a 360-degree environmental awareness.

The 360-degree environmental awareness is something all of us use every day if we drive. Obviously, we use our rearview mirror and side mirrors to create our 360 degrees of awareness. But yes, I know there's always a "blind spot." So what do we do? We turn and look if our vigilance warns us to do so. We all have!

This 360-degree environmental awareness is critical because we are in a potentially deadly weapon, our car – not to mention the cars around us. Most of us got to work or home today using this 360-degree awareness. And then… we parked, got out, locked our car, and forgot about having a 360-degree view of awareness. To increase our safety in the workplace and the life place, we need to increase our awareness of the dangers around us. The 360-degree view of awareness can do this for us!

Developing Escape Plans

When it comes to developing escape plans, keep in mind the following:

Commitment: Look at all your environments and pre-plan your escape routes. Saying you'll do it tomorrow often means someday, which turns into no follow-through.

Involvement: Management should ensure that all staff know the plan. When discussing plans with staff, management should be serious and matter-of-fact. The attitude of leadership when advising departmental staff members should be confident and free of fear.

Practice: Just like your kids do fire drills at school; you should physically and mentally run through the events of your escape. Have a schedule and practice routinely.

"What If?" Game: The "What if?" Game means playing mental scenarios of situations that may arise and force us to take action. The best emergency responders and police officers play the "What if?" game regularly.

Changes: Realize now that things are going to change. You are going to change, and so are most things in life. With this said, doesn't it make sense to update your escape plans as your life changes?

Environments: Environmental Awareness means that you have an understanding of the different types of vulnerabilities and resources in your surroundings.

Relationships: Escape planning always involves more than its physical nature. Successful personal safety involves communication skills that enable us to escape situations involving interpersonal relationships. A sharp awareness is keen to the sharp tongue.

In an active shooter situation,
Rule #1 always escape (RUN) if safe to do so. What if you can't escape? Then we go to Rule #2, HIDE, and Cover. The Federal Government outlines what to do in an active shooter situation. They say, RUN, HIDE, and FIGHT. "Escape if safe to do so" is the RUN part of the run-hide-fight campaign for dealing with an active shooter.

Chapter 9

Hide, Call, Lock, and Barricade

Hide and Cover in Place if You Cannot Escape

Rule #1 (Escape! -RUN) will always be the best response for surviving an active shooter. Unfortunately, we don't always have that option. When faced with a reality of no escape route, we HIDE and cover in place – Rule #2. Once we have hidden or escaped, we will then move to Rule #3 Alert (911), the authorities (police, armed security). Additional considerations when we are hiding is to lock the doors (if they lock) - Rule #4, or place barriers if the doors don't lock – Rule #5.

Rules for Surviving an Active Shooter

1. Escape (RUN) if safe to do so!
2. **HIDE and cover in place if you cannot escape. (SAFE ROOM)**
3. Alert (911) authorities—police, armed security.
4. Lock doors in your immediate area.
5. Place barriers and remain absolutely quiet.
6. If escape is not possible and danger is imminent, (FIGHT) attack the attacker.
7. When law enforcement arrives, be submissive, expose your palms, and do what they tell you to do.

Rule #2 - HIDE and cover in place if you cannot escape.

Right now, if you couldn't escape from the room or area you are in:

- Where would you hide?
- Does your hiding area restrict your movement?
- Would gunshots penetrate your hiding area?
- Do you have a designated Safe Room?

HIDE and Cover in Place if you Cannot Escape. (SAFE ROOM)

Your Hiding Spot Should:

- **Be out of the active shooter's view**
  A hiding spot should be a place where you are not exposed to someone's normal line of sight/vision. Remember hide and seek as a kid. The shooter may try and seek you. You want to be well hidden and out of view.

- **Provide protection if shots are fired**
  There is a difference between concealment and cover. Concealment hides and Cover protects from most projectiles (bullets) coming through the barrier of cover.

- **Not restrict options for movement**
  If the shooter gets in the room you are hiding in, you will want to be able to move and fight (attack (FIGHT) the attacker) if you decide to. Preplanning where you would hide in your environment will help you think through these contingencies.

- **Hide along the wall closest to the exit**
  Hide along the wall closest to the exit but out of view from the hallway and doorway. This position can mitigate the line of fire, should the attacker shoot through the doorway area.

- **Remain silent and in place until the all-clear**
  Remain hidden until law enforcement has given the all-clear.

Use strategies to silently communicate with first responders if possible. Example: in rooms with exterior windows, make signs to silently signal law enforcement and emergency responders to indicate the status of the room's occupants. Be careful not to expose yourself to the active shooter if they are located outside of the environment you are in.

- **Environmental Factors**
  The environment is always a factor. Consider your environment when positioning yourself to hide.

What is in your environment that can help you hide?

- Close blinds and cover windows
- Turn lights off
- Close and lock doors if possible
- Move furniture, equipment, beds, etc. to help you stay hidden
- Silence cell phones
- Crouch down and get as small as possible behind objects
- Consider and understand cover vs. concealment

Alert (911) Authorities—Police, Armed Security

Reporting Scene Information
Law enforcement, first responders, and EMS personnel are responding to a high-risk environment. Any and all information that can be relayed to them prior to entry can be a matter of life or death for them. Thinking through the above elements of reporting scene information is critical. Under stress, many people are confused and disoriented. Proper planning and mental rehearsals can save your life and the lives of others.

Rules for Surviving an Active Shooter

1. Escape (RUN) if safe to do so!
2. HIDE and cover in place if you cannot escape. (SAFE ROOM)
3. **Alert (911) authorities—police, armed security.**
4. Lock doors in your immediate area.
5. Place barriers and remain absolutely quiet.
6. If escape is not possible and danger is imminent, (FIGHT) attack the attacker.
7. When law enforcement arrives, be submissive, expose your palms, and do what they tell you to do.

Rule #3 - Alert (911) authorities—police, armed security.

After you have escaped or hidden, call for help. Very important to follow Rules #1 and #2 first.

- Do you have on-site police/armed security that you can call? If so, do you know the #s?
- If you are calling 911, do you need to dial a number first and then 911?
- Have you ever practiced calling 911 from your cell phone?
- Does your agency have a policy requesting you to call the operator and initiate a code first?

Provide 911 Operators / Law Enforcement with:

- **Location of the shooter(s)**
  911 operators and police will ask you where you are and the location of the shooter. Be aware of your location, landmarks, building, and room numbers.

- **Number of shooters**
  The majority of active shooters have been a lone wolf (one person); however, there could be more than one shooter. This is very important as the police will want to know if there is more than one shooter.

- **Physical description of shooter(s)**

  If the shooter(s) is wearing a black hoodie, camouflage clothing, or dressed in hospital scrubs is important to the police. Identifying the shooter is critical. Are they wearing body armor?

- **Number and types of weapons**

  Attackers use long arms (rifles/shotguns) almost half of the time. Hand guns are most common. Identifying whether the gun is long or short will be valuable to police.

- **Location of the shooter(s) movements and shots fired**

  It will be important to note if the shooter(s) has left the scene and, if so, in which direction are they moving? Also, let authorities know how many shots were fired and when was the last time you heard gunfire should be relayed as well.

- **Number of potential victims and your location**

  If you are fleeing from the scene or hiding in an area and have any information about the number of victims, that will be helpful for police and EMS responders. Noting your immediate location and how many people are with you is important information to relay to law enforcement and 911 operators. Report any knowledge of hostages and location.

Emergency Numbers

_____

_____

_____

_____

Lock Doors in Your Immediate Area

Lock Doors

If you are hiding, it is very important that you lock the doors in your immediate area. Shooters know they are racing against time and probably won't waste too much time trying to get into a locked area.

Rules for Surviving an Active Shooter

1. Escape (RUN) if safe to do so!
2. HIDE and cover in place if you cannot escape. (SAFE ROOM)
3. Alert (911) authorities—police, armed security.
4. **Lock doors in your immediate area.**
5. Place barriers and remain absolutely quiet.
6. If escape is not possible and danger is imminent, (FIGHT) attack the attacker.
7. When law enforcement arrives, be submissive, expose your palms, and do what they tell you to do.

Locking doors and improvising door mechanisms

Having an awareness of the door locks and hardware mechanisms in your environment can save your life. Seconds matter when the armed response is minutes away. Pay attention to how your doors swing (open and close), how they lock (or don't lock), and what can be used to improvise a lock for your doors.

If your doors don't lock...?

Improvise with belts or extension cords on door hardware, lanyards around door mechanisms, door stops, etc.

Place Barriers and Remain Absolutely Quiet

Barriers and Silence

When we cannot escape (run), we hide, call, lock, and barricade. These rules (#2-5) for surviving an active shooter should be followed to give you the best chance of survival. The Federal Government outlines what to do in an active shooter situation. They say RUN, HIDE, and FIGHT. HIDE, Call, and Lock-Barricade is the Hide part of the run-hide-fight campaign for Active Shooter incidents. Barriers and silence may prevent the attacker from getting to you or hearing where you are at.

Rules for Surviving an Active Shooter

1. Escape (RUN) if safe to do so!
2. HIDE and cover in place if you cannot escape. (SAFE ROOM)
3. Alert (911) authorities—police, armed security.
4. Lock doors in your immediate area.
5. **Place barriers and remain absolutely quiet.**
6. If escape is not possible and danger is imminent, (FIGHT) attack the attacker.
7. When law enforcement arrives, be submissive, expose your palms, and do what they tell you to do.

Rule #5 - Place barriers and remain absolutely quiet
Even if your doors lock, you may want to add additional layers of security by placing barricades. If your doors don't lock, barricades are a must.
- What could you use in your environment right now to barricade

the doorway?

- Are you able to move furniture, bookcases, chairs, tables, and office equipment in front of the doorway?
- How fast could you move these items into place to form your barricade?

If the shooter is nearby - Place barriers and remain absolutely quiet

- **Lock the door(s)**
  Always lock doors if/when possible.

- **Barricade from the floor up**
  Use items that are heavy at the base of your barricade.

- **Make it difficult for the attacker to get to you**
  Barricading can buy you time for the police or armed security to arrive. Depending upon how the door(s) swing in or out, the barricade can slow down but not always prevent the attacker's entrance into your environment.

- **Hide behind large item (cabinet, desk)**
  Large items can be used as cover (stops projectiles) and concealment (hides you).

- **Turn the lights out and silence cell phone/pager**
  Getting a call, text message, or email could alert the shooter to your location. Make sure your cell phone is placed on silence. Cell phones are great personal safety tools, but an unwanted sound could compromise your location and alert a shooter to your whereabouts.

- **Remain quiet and alert**
  Stay as calm and quiet as possible. Pray that the shooter does not hear or see you and goes right on by.

- **Prepare to attack the attacker**
  If your barricade does not prohibit the entrance of the attacker, prepare yourself mentally and physically to attack (fight). You may need to act!

Healthcare Barricade Procedures & Guidelines

The decision to stay in an environment where extreme violence is occurring can only be made by the individual. Each person must determine for him or herself if staying to provide care and protect patients or individuals that cannot be moved is prudent for their individual safety.

Steps for remaining in a "hot" zone during an active shooter event.

- Self-awareness and acknowledgement that you may be seriously injured or killed.

- Barricade in areas where patients and non-ambulatory individuals are located.

- Transport patients and non-ambulatory individuals on wheelchairs, stretchers, or by carrying them to a safe location.

- Identify a safe location in your unit before an event, where staff and patients may safely barricade themselves during the incident.

- If the shooter is not located in your unit, learn how to lock down and barricade your unit in case of an attempt to enter the unit during an active shooter incident.

- Provide emergency numbers at all available phone lines.

Facility Lockdown - Healthcare Agencies and Corporations

Pre-planned External Lockdown and Traffic Control
Prior to an active shooter incident, law enforcement and security should coordinate and develop a plan for the external lockdown of a healthcare facility or corporation.

The Facility Lockdown Plan Should Include:

- Lockdown and control access procedures.

- Notification to EMS regarding the lockdown and patient diversion.

- Evacuation of non-impacted, non-medical areas such as waiting areas, cafeterias, chapels, etc.

- Movement of patients, staff, and visitors to safe locations.

- Providing supplies, equipment, pharmaceuticals, water, and food to lockdown areas.

- Facility census, updates, and reporting in coordination with the lockdown.

- Coordination and diversion of incoming traffic to other healthcare facilities.

- Communication with staff and law enforcement inside the healthcare/corporate facility.

Chapter 10

Attack the Attacker

Rule #6 LAST RESORT! If escape is not possible and danger is imminent, attack (FIGHT) the attacker. Escape will always be the best response for surviving an active shooter. HIDE will always be the second-best response for surviving an active shooter. Unfortunately, we may not have either option. When faced with the reality of no escape route and no place to hide and cover, we have a choice. We fight (attack the attacker), and maybe we get injured or die. Or, we don't fight (attack the attacker) and injury and/or death are absolute. If we fight (attack the attacker), at least we have a chance. It's a decision that no one can make for another person. Only YOU can decide! I (the author) have made my decision, and hopefully, this chapter will help you make yours.

Rules for Surviving an Active Shooter

1. Escape (RUN) if safe to do so!
2. HIDE and cover in place if you cannot escape. (SAFE ROOM)
3. Alert (911) authorities—police, armed security.
4. Lock doors in your immediate area.
5. Place barriers and remain absolutely quiet.
6. **If escape is not possible and danger is imminent, (FIGHT) attack the attacker.**
7. When law enforcement arrives, be submissive, expose your palms, and do what they tell you to do.

Rule #6 - If escape is not possible and danger is imminent, attack (FIGHT) the attacker.

Right now, you are in a situation where danger is imminent (you hear the gunshots getting closer), and you have nowhere to escape to or hide.

- **What would you do?**
    - ○ Do you fight (attack (FIGHT) the attacker)?
    - ○ Do you submit (not fight, and hope nothing happens)?
- If you decide to fight (attack (FIGHT) the attacker), are you fully committed?
- If you decide to fight (attack (FIGHT) the attacker), what are some weapons that are available to you in your environment?
- Where would you position yourself to attack (FIGHT) the attacker?
- Are there others with you, and are they willing to attack (FIGHT) the attacker with you?
- Where and how would you strike the attacker?

If escape is not possible and danger is imminent, attack (FIGHT) the attacker.

As an absolute last resort: (self-defense is always—always—last resort)

- **Act as aggressively as possible**
  Most people are just not aggressive. So how do you just all of a sudden get aggressive? You don't! You will need to mentally prepare yourself ahead of time to act with aggression. Mental Movies and Impressing the Unconscious Mind will be discussed in this chapter. The mental component of attacking the attacker is the most important aspect of engaging in this last resort option.

- **Swarm! If there is more than one of you.**
  To swarm is to attack the attacker simultaneously with more than one person. Obviously, you cannot demand that others attack the attacker with you, but you can encourage them. This last resort

option is up to each individual. This is why training and mental preparations are so important for everyone in your workplace/society. When we swarm and attack the attacker, it may cause a momentary distraction, which buys us time to incapacitate him. The following tactics will assist us as we swarm and attack the attacker.

- **Improvise weapons and throw items**
  There are many weapons more than likely in your environment right now. You just might not realize that. Improvised weapons are anything that can be picked up and thrown or used to strike the attacker. We will examine dangerous weapons in your environment further in this chapter.

- **Yell and Scream!**
  Using a loud scream or yell can cause a momentary delay. Momentary delays are distractions. Distractions affect the senses, and it takes time for the mind to process the new information. They mainly affect a person's sight and sense of hearing; however, psychological distractions, such as asking a person something completely out of the ordinary, can cause a mental delay as well. Distractions have been used since ancient times and are a valuable advantage you should always consider using.

- **Strike to High-Risk Target Areas**
  When striking the human body, different levels of resultant trauma may vary dependent on where you strike the individual. An active shooter is using deadly force; therefore, it is recommended that you strike areas that are "high-risk target areas." Striking any area other than a high-risk target area is a waste of time and energy and may expose you to increased danger. The high-risk target areas will be examined in this chapter.

- **Commit to your actions!**
  Anything less than a 100% commitment is also a waste of time

and energy and could expose you to increased danger. In an active shooter situation, we must have an attitude of "How dare you affect my life this way!" "How dare you take my life!" "How dare you affect my children's future!" The "how dare you" attitude creates a mindset of full commitment to our actions and livelihood.

- **This is not a recommendation to attack (fight) but rather a choice to attack (fight) where there are no other options.**
  You have a choice: live or die, fight or not fight. No one will force you to fight (attack the attacker) but you. The public safety "golden rule" is…at the end of the shift, we go home. The caveat to this rule is: We go home in the same condition that we started in, if not better. Make the choice that YOU are going home. Remember, attack (FIGHT) is not a recommendation; it is a choice. You choose!

Duck and Cover

YES or NO? Is duck and cover a good option/choice?

Yes, if the shooter is nowhere near the area and you are hiding, barricaded in, and have called for help. Then yes, it would be ok.

No, it would not be ok if you can't completely hide and barricade, and there is a possibility that the shooter gets in the area you are in. Duck and cover can then end up as a sitting duck, which could lead to a dead duck. Duck and cover do not give a person an opportunity to attack (FIGHT) the attacker if they are faced with that type of situation.

Attack (FIGHT) Disclaimer

Personal Safety Training Inc. makes no legal declaration, representation, or claim as to what force should be used or not used during an active shooter situation or a self-defense or assault incident or situation. Each individual must take into consideration their ability, agency policies and procedures, and laws in the state and country in which they reside.

Attack (FIGHT) the Attacker with weapons and improvised weapons/items you can throw at the attacker.

Clubs and Sticks are available in most work environments. They are broom and mop handles, crutches, canes, walkers, umbrellas, and/or anything that is an extension of the hand. These weapons and improvised weapons can be used to incapacitate the attacker. Strike high-risk target areas with clubs and sticks.

Knives/Edged or Sharpened Weapons are also available in most environments. Kitchen utensils can be utilized, as well as any other sharp object. Clip-it knives and common kitchen knives could be available. These weapons and improvised weapons can be used to incapacitate the attacker.

Thrown Objects Like the above weapons and improvised weapons, a thrown object (chair, table, computer, etc.) can seriously injure the attacker. This also gives you some distance between yourself and the attacker. These weapons and improvised weapons can be used to incapacitate the attacker.

Guns: Law Enforcement's response will be to use their guns (firearms) to stop the attacker. In some instances, staff, visitors, or others (security) may have a gun (concealed permit), which could be used to stop the attacker. One must consider that others (besides the shooter) may be shot if the person using the gun to stop the shooter hits others (collateral damage).

These weapons and other improvised weapons can be used to incapacitate the attacker.

Weapons at hand in YOUR workplace: Learn the best way to attack using regular items that can suddenly become a weapon.

Attack (FIGHT) the Attacker with Improvised Weapons

- **Pens**
  A pen can easily impale the human body. Pens are a common tool that we all use. Increase your awareness by knowing that you may need to use your pen as a weapon against the attacker. These weapons and improvised weapons can be used to incapacitate the attacker.

- **Other Edged Weapons: scissors, kitchen utensils, etc.**
  Be aware that edged weapons are almost everywhere in the workplace environment. Kitchen utensils and office items are common in most work environments and may be used in a defensive situation. These weapons and improvised weapons can be used to incapacitate the attacker.

- **Items that can be moved or picked up.**
  Anything that can be picked up can be used as a weapon—staplers, heavy binders, small copiers, etc. These weapons and improvised weapons can be used to incapacitate the attacker.

- **Fire Extinguishers**
  Fire extinguishers are common in most workplaces. The propellant, when sprayed to the face of the attacker, will cake into the eyes and take their breath away. The cylinder can be

used to incapacitate the attacker as well. Prior knowledge of using an extinguisher is very important.

- **Glass/Beverages**
  Glass and other hard items that hold beverages and food can be thrown or used to

Strike (Attack) High-Risk Target Areas

When using any weapon, improvised or other—including your human body—as a personal defensive weapon, you will want to ensure that your strikes (attacks) are effective by targeting them toward a high-risk area of the human body. Striking any other area may not be effective!

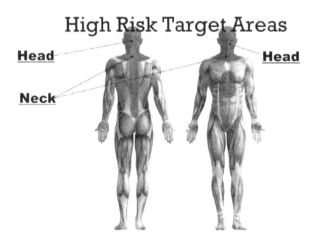

High Risk Target Areas

Head Head

Neck

The High-Risk Target areas of the human body to be targeted on the attacker are the: HEAD, NECK, and upper SPINE of the attacker.

- High-Risk Target Areas are for situations where the subject is using force that is likely to cause serious injury or death to one or more people.

- Force-directed to High-Risk Target Areas may cause a greater risk of injury to the subject. Individuals must be justified and reasonable in using deadly force against a subject.

- The level of resultant trauma to these areas tends to be serious and/or long-lasting. Injury to the subject may include serious bodily injury, unconsciousness, shock, or death.

- Without this knowledge and understanding of where to strike, your interventions could be ineffective and expose you to an increased risk of injury and/or death.

The Federal Government outlines what to do in an active shooter situation. They say, **RUN, HIDE, and FIGHT**.

Attack the Attacker is the Fight part of the run-hide-fight campaign for active shooter incidents.

Mental Movies - Impressing the Unconscious Mind

As humans, we have the ability to pre-play events in our minds. We also have the ability to replay past events in our minds. Most people have experienced both facets of playing mental movies and impressing the non-conscious mind. Unfortunately, most people spend far more energy pre-playing negative events (worry) and re-playing negative events (from the past that were negative) than visualizing positive outcomes.

One of the most important aspects of preparing for and surviving an active shooter event is your mental preparedness. Imagining and visualizing your successful response to an active shooter incident is vital to your safety and survival.

Mental Movies - Impressing the Unconscious Mind

- **Stage 1:** Create the scene of the event, incident, or situation in your mind's eye.

- **Stage 2:** Make the scene as clear and colorful as possible. Focus your mind's eye as you create this clear, concise mental scene.

- **Stage 3:** "Lights, Focus, Camera, and Action!" Now that the scene is clear and focused, give it action. As the director of your mental movie, you direct everything in it.

- **Stage 4:** The plot/outcome is up to you! You decide what happens when it happens and who it happens to. You are the hero of your mental movie. You always win in your mind's eye when you create, direct, and choreograph the mental movie.

- **Stage 5**: Feel what it is like to be the star of your mental movie. Positive energy helps build, reinforce, and utilize the mental power we all have. This ultimately makes us stronger, more decisive, and automatic in our responses.

- **Stage 6:** Remember to pre-play your mental movie to prepare for possible future situations. We are the only creature with this ability. Re-play positive outcomes and try not to re-play negative outcomes of real situations. If you do re-play negative situations in your mind's eye, make sure to always change the outcome to your choosing.

Chapter 11

Law Enforcement, Post-Incident Responses & Documentation

Rule #7 Law Enforcement's Response
Almost every law enforcement agency is trained to respond to an active shooter situation. Training for law enforcement continues to evolve and expand based on this increasing high-level threat to the civilian population. Officer tactics/strategies for responding and dealing with an active shooter have advanced as well.

Law enforcement's immediate purpose in an active shooter incident/event is to STOP the shooter.

Rules for Surviving an Active Shooter

1. Escape (RUN) if safe to do so!
2. HIDE and cover in place if you cannot escape. (SAFE ROOM)
3. Alert (911) authorities—police, armed security.
4. Lock doors in your immediate area.
5. Place barriers and remain absolutely quiet.
6. If escape is not possible and danger is imminent, (FIGHT) attack the attacker.
7. **When law enforcement arrives, be submissive, expose your palms, and do what they tell you to do.**

Law Enforcement's Immediate Priority in an Active Shooter Incident is to:

- **Stop the Active Shooter!**
  Police officers today are trained to and prepared to move

towards the sound of gunfire and violence. Officers put their lives on the line to keep us safe and save human lives. If the shooter is actively engaged in killing others and not surrendering, police will use deadly force to stop the attacker.

- **Proceed to the area where the last gunshots were heard.**
  Even though the shots have stopped, that doesn't mean the violence is over. Police will, however, respond to the area where the shots were last heard. Based on information known about active shooters, most will end the violence themselves by committing suicide. They know that police will respond and use deadly force. Some shooters will commit suicide by forcing the police to shoot them, also known as suicide by cop.

- **Eliminate the threat**
  The priority of law enforcement is to eliminate the threat. Once the threat is eliminated, no more people will be killed or injured. It is a serious and emergent response to a deadly situation. Some police agencies will have special entry teams, sometimes called SWAT or other tactical response entry teams.

Police/Armed Security Entry Teams

Armed Response Teams May:

- **Wear bulletproof vests, helmets, and other tactical equipment.** Entry teams and those specialized in special weapons and tactics may be wearing tactical gear. Their gear may be all black, or they may be camouflaged with helmets and face coverings. Their appearance and tactical movement may scare staff.
  - Having knowledge of this can mitigate staff anxiety.

- **Be armed with rifles, shotguns, and/or handguns.**
Law enforcement will always be armed with at least a handgun—many agencies today outfit patrol officers and other police responders with rifles, and some with shotguns.

- **Shout verbal commands!**
The stress that armed response teams will be experiencing will be hard to imagine. They are putting their lives on the line to protect the public. Officers will be loud and will shout verbal commands to individuals. Obey their verbal commands! They may yell at you to do what they need you to do.

- **Push individuals to the ground for their safety.** More than likely, officers will shout verbal commands for you to move, go to the ground, put your hands up, etc. They may push you to the ground for their safety and for yours. Remember, their number one priority is to STOP the active shooter. Their actions may seem aggressive, but they are doing what they are trained to do. Comply with their commands. You do not want to be mistaken for an aggressive individual.

Police/Armed Security Arrival

- **Drop any items in your hands.**
Police and security officers are trained to watch the hands—because what is in the hands can hurt them or kill them. Make sure your hands are visible, and there is nothing in them. Drop your purse, bag, or anything in your hands. You do not want any item to be mistaken for a weapon of some sort.

- **Raise hands and spread fingers.**
With your hands raised and fingers spread open, there will be no reason to believe that YOU are a danger to the police. This message is universally accepted as a sign of submission.

- **Remain calm and DO WHAT THEY TELL YOU!**
  This can't be overemphasized. Do what they tell you to do!

- **Avoid quick or sudden movements.**
  Any quick or sudden movement could be mistaken as an act of aggression. Law enforcement officers do not know what type of hostile environment they may be moving into. Display submission!

- **Avoid pointing, screaming, or yelling.**
  Pointing, screaming, and yelling may be confusing to the officers and appear aggressive. Do your best to avoid this behavior. Mentally preparing yourself ahead of time (mental movies and impressing the unconscious mind) is imperative.

- **Proceed in the direction from which officers are entering.**
  Whichever way the officers are coming from will be safe. They may or may not direct you in that direction. They may want you to stay put. Whatever they want you to do, do it!

- **Go to a Safe Location!**
  If law enforcement directs you to leave, obviously, go to a safe location. Your agency may mandate this in policy and procedures for emergent situations such as active shooter, fire, hazmat, tornado, earthquake, etc. Law enforcement may override this and have you go to their directed area.

Go to a Safe Location, an area controlled by law enforcement until:

- **The situation is under control.**
  A location controlled by law enforcement will be an area where they can effectively account for staff and possible subjects, accomplices, or individuals of interest.

- **All witnesses are identified and questioned.**
  An active shooter situation is a crime scene, and appropriate police protocols for an investigation must be followed.

- **They release you to leave the area.**
  Obviously, you will be frightened and concerned about letting your loved ones know that you are all right. The importance of maintaining your composure and working with law enforcement will not only be appreciated; it will be expected.

- **Healthcare personnel may be needed to return to their assignments.**
  Healthcare personnel who have evacuated from an active shooter incident and are staged in a safe location will be released to provide emergent/patient care to those in need.

- **Notify loved ones of your location and safety.**
  Instantly because of social media and 24hr news networks, an active shooter incident is broadcast. Your friends and family will be beyond worried if the event is at your workplace. A text message and/or phone call will be appreciated by all.

- **Caution: compromising a crime scene.**
  An active shooter incident/event is a crime scene, and evidence will need to be preserved for appropriate prosecution of those involved.

Risk Management for Liability Mitigation

Post-incident documentation is always critical for reducing your exposure and risk of litigation. The above recommendations for post-incident documentation can assist legal, risk management, and corporate staff in potential legal proceedings. An active shooter incident would be horrendous for any individual and/or agency to deal with. Unfortunately, it is a reality for some, and with that reality comes the importance of documentation.

Post-Incident Documentation

- **Who-What-Where-When-Why-How**
  The first rule in post-incident documentation is the "who, what, where, when, why, and how" rule of reporting. After writing an incident narrative, double-check to see if you have included the first rule of reporting.

- **Witnesses (who was there?)**
  Make sure to include anyone who was a witness to the incident. Staff, visitors, guests, and support services (police, fire, EMS, etc.) can be valuable witnesses should an incident be litigated.

- **Narrative Characteristics**
  A proper narrative should describe in detail the characteristics of the violent incident.

- **Before, During, and After**
  A thorough incident report will describe what happened before, during, and after the incident. Details matter!

- **1st Person vs. 3rd Person**
  The account of an incident can be described in the first person or third person. This can be specific to your agency protocols or the preference of the person documenting the incident.

- **Post-Follow-Up (track and trend)**
  Most agencies use electronic documentation, which allows for easy retrieval, tracking, and trending. Using technology assists agencies to follow up and initiate proactive corrections.

- **Follow Standard Operating Procedures**
  Whether it is handwriting incident reports or electronic documentation and charting, staff should consistently and thoroughly document all incidents relating to violence in the workplace.

Elements of Reporting Self-Defense or Force

Report and Document
After any situation involving the defense of yourself or another person, proper documentation and reporting are crucial. The events of the assault or attempted assault should be reported to security/police. The police/security will document the incident and start an investigation. You should also document the account for your own internal records. This can protect you in a possible legal situation that could arise out of using force to defend yourself. As you document your account of the incident, make sure to report to security/police any details you missed during your initial report to them.

What type of force/self-defense was used during the incident?
Be specific in your documentation regarding the type of control, defense, and force that was used during the incident.

How long did the incident and resistance last?
It is important to note the length of the resistance, as this is a factor relative to exhaustion and increasing the level of force.

Were you in fear of injury (bodily harm) to yourself, others, or the subject?
Fear is a distressing emotion aroused by a perceived threat, impending danger, evil, or pain.
- **If so, Why?**

Fear is a basic survival mechanism occurring in response to a specific stimulus, such as pain or the threat of danger.

Thoroughly explain, and make sure to document completely.
The importance of documentation cannot be overemphasized. Documentation ensures proper training standards are met, policies and procedures are understood, certification standards are met, liability and risk management mitigation, and departmental and organizational requirements are maintained.

Special Note

Every person must take into consideration their moral, legal, and ethical beliefs, rights, and understandings when using any type of force to defend themselves or others. Personal Safety Training Inc. makes no legal declaration, representation, or claim as to what force should be used or not used during a self-defense/assault incident or situation. Each trainee must take into consideration their ability, agency policies and procedures, and state and federal laws.

Chapter 12

Stop the Bleed

The **'Stop the Bleed' campaign** was initiated by a federal interagency workgroup convened by the National Security Council Staff, The White House. The purpose of the campaign is to build national resilience by better preparing the public to save lives by raising awareness of basic actions to stop life-threatening bleeding following everyday emergencies and man-made and natural disasters. Advances made by military medicine and research in hemorrhage control during the wars in Afghanistan and Iraq have informed the work of this initiative, which exemplifies translation of knowledge back to the homeland to the benefit of the general public.

The Department of Defense owns the 'Stop the Bleed' logo and phrase – trademark pending. AVADE® Active Shooter Training supports the efforts of this campaign and is committed to equipping YOU to save your own life and possibly the lives of others.

How to Stop the Bleed - Call 9-1-1

- Call 9-1-1 yourself

  OR

- Tell someone to call 9-1-1

Ensure Your Safety

- Before you offer any help, you must ensure your own safety!

- If you become injured, you will not be able to help the victim.

- Provide care to the injured person if the scene is safe for you to do so. If, at any time, your safety is threatened, attempt to remove yourself (and the victim if possible) from danger and find a safe location.

- Protect yourself from blood-borne infections by wearing gloves, if available.

Look for Life-Threatening Bleeding

- Find the source of bleeding

- Open or remove the clothing over the wound so you can clearly see it. By removing clothing, you will be able to see injuries that may have been hidden or covered.

- Look for and identify "life-threatening" bleeding.

    o Examples include:
        - Blood that is spurting out of the wound.
        - Blood that won't stop coming out of the wound.
        - Blood that is pooling on the ground.
        - Clothing that is soaked with blood.
        - Bandages that are soaked with blood.
        - Loss of all or part of an arm or leg.
        - Bleeding in a victim who is now confused or unconscious.

Compress and Control

There are a number of methods that can be used to stop bleeding, and they all have one thing in common—compressing a bleeding blood vessel in order to stop the bleeding.

If you DON'T have a trauma first aid kit:

Apply direct pressure on the wound. (Cover the wound with a clean cloth and apply pressure by pushing directly on it with both hands.)

1. Take any clean cloth (for example, a shirt) and cover the wound.
2. If the wound is large and deep, try to "stuff" the cloth down into the wound.
3. Apply continuous pressure with both hands directly on top of the bleeding wound.
4. Push down as hard as you can.
5. Hold pressure to stop bleeding. Continue pressure until relieved by medical responders.

If you DO have a trauma first aid kit:

For life-threatening bleeding from an arm or leg when a tourniquet is NOT available OR for bleeding from the neck, shoulder, or groin:

- Pack (stuff) the wound with a bleeding control (also called a hemostatic) gauze, plain gauze, or a clean cloth, and then apply pressure with both hands

1. Open the clothing over the bleeding wound.
2. Wipe away any pooled blood.
3. Pack (stuff) the wound with bleeding control gauze (preferred), plain gauze, or a clean cloth.
4. Apply steady pressure with both hands directly on top of the bleeding wound.
5. Push down as hard as you can.
6. Hold pressure to stop bleeding. Continue pressure until relieved by medical responders.

Uncontrolled bleeding is a major cause of preventable deaths. Approximately 40% of trauma-related deaths worldwide are due to bleeding or its consequences, establishing hemorrhage as the most common cause of preventable death in trauma.[5]

---

[5] * Curry N, Hopewell S, Doree C, Hyde C, Brohi K, Stanworth S. The acute management of trauma hemorrhage: a systematic review of randomized controlled trials. Crit Care. 2011;15(2):R92.

Tourniquets

For life-threatening bleeding from an arm or leg when a tourniquet is available:

- ▪ Applying the tourniquet[6]

1. Wrap the tourniquet around the bleeding arm or leg about 2 to 3 inches above the bleeding site (be sure NOT to place the tourniquet onto a joint—go above the joint if necessary)

2. Pull the free end of the tourniquet to make it as tight as possible and secure the free end.

3. Twist or wind the windlass until the bleeding stops.

4. Secure the windlass to keep the tourniquet tight.

5. Note the time the tourniquet was applied.

Note: A tourniquet will cause pain, but it is necessary to stop life-threatening bleeding.

---

[6] Pons PT, Jacobs L. Save a life: What everyone should know to stop bleeding after an injury. Chicago, IL: American College of Surgeons; 2016.

SAVE A LIFE

BLEEDINGCONTROL.ORG

1 APPLY PRESSURE WITH HANDS

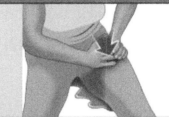

2 APPLY DRESSING AND PRESS

3 APPLY TOURNIQUET

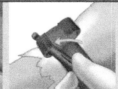

| WRAP | WIND | SECURE | TIME |

CALL 911

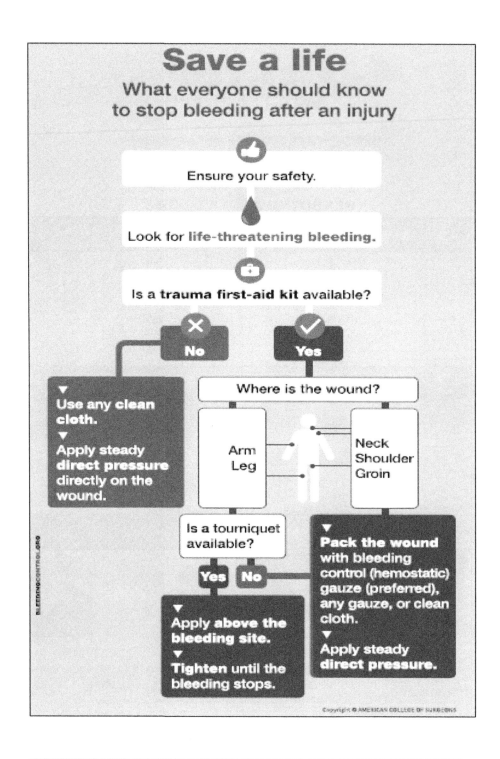

Chapter 13

Honoring the Victims and Heroes

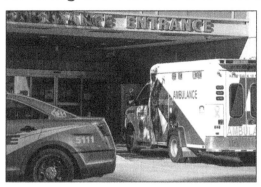

So much emphasis on active shooter incidents is placed on the perpetrators. And we know that is just what they want. We need to shift this emphasis to honoring the victims and heroes of an active shooter incident.

The Victims/Heroes of Active Shooter Incidents—Who are they?

- **Victims/Heroes (Survivors and Non-Survivors**
- **Civilian Interveners**
- **Police (on and off duty)**
- **EMS/FIRE Personnel**
- **Healthcare Personnel**
- **Trainers/Teachers**
- **State and Federal Organizations**
- **YOU, for being willing to act - and help others.**

Victims and Heroes—Every day people who are heroes and victims don't wear red capes and have their names plastered on billboards and across the internet for all to see. They are people just like you and me. There is not a lot written about them other than a few stray articles and numbers called statistics.

Rachel Joy Scott

(August 5, 1981 – April 20, 1999)

An American student, author, and the first victim of the Columbine High School massacre, in which eleven other students and a teacher were also murdered before both perpetrators committed suicide.

She was posthumously the subject and co-writer of several books and the inspiration for Rachel's Challenge, an international school outreach program and the most popular school assembly program in America. Its aim is to advocate Scott's values, based on her life, her journals, and the contents of a two-page essay, penned a month before her murder, entitled My Ethics; My Codes of Life. The essay advocates her belief in compassion being "the greatest form of love humans have to offer." https://rachelschallenge.org

Thousands of people have been killed and injured by active shooters. But how about the number of people who were affected by the extreme violence of an active shooter? That number may never be known. The families, wives, husbands, sons, daughters, moms, dads, siblings, aunts, uncles, friends, associates, co-workers, etc. that are affected by active shooter/extreme violence are beyond what we can imagine. - My heart goes out to ALL of you!

Civilian Interveners and Police (on and off duty)

Joel Myrick

Pearl, Mississippi—A shooter fatally stabbed his mother at home before opening fire at his high school, killing two students and injuring seven others. The attack was stopped when Assistant Principal Joel Myrick retrieved his .45 caliber handgun from his truck and confronted the shooter, detaining him until authorities could arrive. Myrick's action stopped the shooter from going across the street to the middle school as he had planned.

James Strand

Parker Middle School—A 14-year-old student showed up at his middle school dance carrying a .25-caliber pistol. He opened fire inside the dance, killing one teacher and wounding another as well as two students. The rampage ended when James Strand, owner of the banquet hall the dance was happening in, grabbed his personal shotgun, and confronted the 14-year-old killer. Strand held the teen at gunpoint for 11 minutes before finally getting him to drop the weapon and lie on the ground and searching him for additional weapons.

Gross and Bridges

Appalachian School of Law—A 43-year-old former student, armed with a .380 handgun, killed two persons with point-blank shots and went on to kill fellow students as well as wounding three others before being confronted at gunpoint by law student Tracy Bridges, a county sheriff's deputy, and Mikael Gross, a police officer, after retrieving their personal handguns from their vehicles. The gunman was then apprehended by other students.

Jeanne Assam

The shooter opens fire at the Youth with a Mission training center in Arvada, Colorado, with a pistol, killing two and wounding two others before escaping. Later that afternoon, he attacked the New Life Church in Colorado Springs, Colorado, with a number of firearms, killing two more people and injuring three before being shot by Jeanne Assam, a member of the church's safety team, who had been carrying a concealed firearm. The shooter subsequently died from a gunshot to the head, which was inflicted either by himself or by Assam.

Aaron Guyton

Freewill Baptist Church—Aaron Guyton was inside the recreation building of his grandfather's church when he saw the shooter, a member of the congregation, pulling a shotgun from his vehicle. Guyton leaped into action, locking the doors to the church where services were going on. The shooter kicked in the door and pointed the shotgun at Rev. Henry Guyton and several parishioners. Drawing his concealed handgun, the younger Guyton held Gates at gunpoint while two members of the church took him to the ground. Rev. Guyton then took the shotgun from his hand.

Nick Meli
Clackamas Town Center Mall—Two people were killed, and a third was seriously wounded at this mall near Portland, Oregon, when a rifle-toting gunman opened fire in the busy food court. Nick Meli, a shopper in the mall, drew a personally owned firearm on the gunman, who immediately retreated to a service corridor and killed himself. Meli did not fire his weapon for fear of striking bystanders, yet authorities say his actions caused the gunman to cease his attack and end his own life.

Correctional Officers
Cache Valley Hospital—Armed with two handguns, a man entered the Cache Valley Hospital emergency room and began making demands. After demanding to see a doctor, he racked the slide on one of his handguns and told hospital employees, "someone is going to die today." While a security guard tried to keep the gunman's focus on him, two corrections officers who happened to be at the hospital on an unrelated matter engaged from another direction. The gunman was shot three times, and no other people were harmed.

Uber Driver Critically Wounds Chicago Gunman
The shooter opens fire on a crowd milling about Logan Square. The Uber driver took out his concealed carry pistol and judiciously hit the shooter several times, disabling him from further engaging bystanders. Chicago police arrived to find the shooter struck several times from gunshot wounds originating from the Uber driver. The driver was released without charges. No bystanders were hit by bullets, and no other injuries were reported in connection with this event.

Jon Meis, Security Guard
Seattle Pacific University—Jon Meis had a habit of carrying pepper

spray that may have saved students' lives after a man opened fire at SEAPAC. The shooter had just wounded three people, one of whom died. He was reloading his shotgun when Meis, a volunteer security guard, saw an opening. He doused the gunman with the spray and tackled him to the ground. Other students at Seattle Pacific University piled on and took the weapon away from the shooter. Officers are convinced the bloodshed at the school would have been worse had Meis and the others not intervened.

Mark Vaughan
Moore, Oklahoma—A man went berserk in a food plant and attacked a female worker, literally decapitating her. He then went after a second woman. Hearing the screams, Chief Operating Officer Mark Vaughan availed himself of a firearm, ran to the scene, and shot down the killer.

Off-Duty Police Officer
Aurora, Colorado—A crazed gunman showed up at a church and opened fire, killing one woman. Before he could claim any more victims, however, he was shot and killed by an off-duty police officer among the parishioners, who was carrying his own handgun. The incident occurred at the New Destiny Christian Center.

Off-Duty Police Officer
Salt Lake City, Utah—Kenneth Hammond was having dinner with his wife in a mall restaurant when he heard the shots and responded. The shooter had killed five helpless victims and wounded four when Hammond spotted him and opened fire with his handgun. The incident ended there—Hammond pinned the gunman in position until the first responding officer arrived. The gunman was eventually killed by SWAT officers.

Police Officer
Three people were killed and 14 injured after a gunman drove through two Kansas towns taking shots at people before opening fire at his workplace. The rampage was stopped by a single officer who braved incoming fire to engage and kill the gunman. By the time the first

police officer arrived at the scene, the gunman was actively shooting at any targets that came into his sights.

EMS/FIRE Personnel

Extraordinary efforts on the part of local Fire and EMS agencies and direct pre-planned coordination with law enforcement are required during a response to an active shooter incident in order to rapidly effect a rescue, save lives, and enable operations with mitigated risk to personnel. Today, EMTs and paramedics need to be ready to respond to an active-shooter incident. EMS and Fire Rescue agency personnel are heroes who lay down their lives to rescue, save, and treat victims of an active shooter incident.

Healthcare Personnel

Most all violence ends up at the hospital. Emergency department personnel, physicians, and many others in healthcare are absolutely critical for dealing with traumas and life-threatening injuries. We cannot express the full measure of our praise and gratitude to you, who selflessly provide care and compassion to those in need. Thank you!

Trainers/Teachers/Educators

For all of you, the teachers and trainers providing education on how to survive and respond to an active shooter incident, my hat goes off to each and every one of you!

A special thanks to:

- All of our certified AVADE® Instructors. **Thank YOU for what you do!**
- For all of the Police/Law Enforcement trainers.
- For the Dads and Moms who share with their children what to do in the event of extreme violence.
- All of the teachers in all of our schools and universities who educate their students on active shooter survival and response.

The following organizations/ training programs also deserve a special thank you:

- **Dept. of Homeland Security** https://www.dhs.gov/active-shooter-preparedness
- **FBI** https://www.fbi.gov/about/partnerships/office-of-partner-engagement/active-shooter-incidents
- **FEMA** ttps://training.fema.gov/is/courseoverview.aspx?code=IS-907
- **RUN-HIDE-FIGHT**
  https://www.youtube.com/watch?v=5VcSwejU2D0
- **(ALERRT)** The Advanced Law Enforcement Rapid Response Training - http://alerrt.org/
- **AVADE® Active Shooter** www.avadeactiveshooter.com

Thank YOU (the reader) for being willing to act - and help others.

My hope, my wish, prayer, my everything is that YOU will be ready and willing to ACT if you ever need to. This book is for you, the everyday person, worker, family man/woman, and child who doesn't have a gun (or who does have a gun) and is willing to confront violence with a plan and strategy. Does that mean you need to stop the violence? No. What it means is you need to stay alive. Staying alive means we escape if we can, we hide if we can't escape, we alert those with the tactics and skills to confront the violence (police-armed security), and we attack (FIGHT) the attacker if we have no other options. It is absolutely sad that a book/training program like this is needed, but I am absolutely glad that you have decided to read it. Without knowledge, awareness, and understanding, we perish.

Hosea 4:6 " My people are destroyed for lack of knowledge: because thou hast rejected knowledge, I will also reject thee, that thou shalt be no priest to me: seeing thou hast forgotten the law of thy God, I will also forget thy children" (KJV)

God Bless YOU!

–David Fowler

About the Author

David Fowler is the founder and president of (PSTI) Personal Safety Training Incorporated and AVADE® Training, located in Coeur d' Alene, ID. He is responsible for the overall management and operations of PSTI and AVADE®, which offers seminars, training, consulting, and protective details. Since 1990, David has been involved in security operations, training, and protective details.

He is the author of the SOCS® (Safety Oriented Customer Service) program and training manual, as well as the AVADE® Personal Safety Training and Workplace Violence Prevention programs and training manuals. He is also the author of the book Be Safe Not Sorry - The art and science of keeping YOU and your family safe from crime and violence. David has worked with thousands of individuals and hundreds of agencies and corporations throughout the United States and Canada. His presentations have included international, national, and local seminars. David's thorough understanding of safety and security, as well as martial science, adds an exciting and interesting approach to his style of presentation.

David is a certified master instructor in several nationally recognized training programs such as Workplace Violence Prevention (AVADE®), Pepper Spray Defense™, Handcuffing Tactics™, Security Oriented Customer Service (SOCS®), Defensive Tactics System™ (DTS™), Defense Baton™, Security Incident Reporting System™ (SIRS™), and AVADE® Personal Safety Training. David has certified and trained thousands of individuals in these programs and others throughout the United States and abroad.

He is a graduate of (ESI) Executive Security International's Advanced Executive Protection Program and the Protective Intelligence and Investigations program. He is also a member of ASIS (American Society for Industrial Security), The International Law Enforcement Educators & Trainers Association (ILEETA), and the International Association of Healthcare Safety & Security (IAHSS).

David brings insight, experience, and a passion for empowering people and organizations utilizing the training programs and protective services that he offers here in the United States and in other countries. He is considered by many to be the most dynamic and motivational speaker and trainer in the security and personal safety industry.

David is happily married to the love of his life, Genelle Fowler. They live in Coeur d' Alene, ID, and have five children and two grandchildren. David and Genelle have committed their lives to serving others through the mission of safety. Both David and Genelle travel extensively, providing training and consulting to corporations throughout North America.

Bibliography, Reference Guide, and Recommended Reading

ASIS International. Security Management Magazine.
www.securitymanagment.com 2006-2016.

DeBecker, Gavin. The Gift of Fear.
Dell Publishing, NY, NY 1997.

Fowler, David. Be Safe Not Sorry, the Art and Science of keeping
YOU and YOUR FAMILY SAFE from Crime and Violence.
Personal Safety Training Inc., Coeur d Alene, ID 2011.

Fowler, David. Violence In The Workplace: Education, Prevention &
Mitigation.
Personal Safety Training Inc., Coeur d Alene, ID 2012.

Fowler, David. Violence In The Workplace II: Education, Prevention
& Mitigation Strategies, and Techniques.
Personal Safety Training Inc., Coeur d Alene, ID 2016.

Fowler, David. Violence In The Workplace III: Education, Prevention
& Mitigation Strategies, and Techniques.
Personal Safety Training Inc., Coeur d Alene, ID 2018.

Fowler, David. To Serve and Protect: Providing SERVICE while
maintaining SAFETY in the Workplace.
Personal Safety Training Inc., Coeur d Alene, ID 2015

Fowler, David. SURVIVE an Active Shooter: Awareness,
Preparedness, and Response for EXTREME VIOLENCE.
Personal Safety Training Inc., Coeur d Alene, ID 2018.

Kinnaird, Brian. Use of Force: Expert Guidance for Decisive Force
Response.
Looseleaf Law Publications, Flushing, NY 2003.

Loehr, James, and Migdwo, Jeffrey. Breathe In Breathe Out: Inhale Energy and Exhale Stress By Guiding and Controlling Your Breathing. Time-Life Books, Alexandria, VI 1986

Personal Safety Training Inc. AVADE® Instructor Manual. 2020

Websites and Weblinks

http://www.AVADEtraining.com

http://www.personalsafetytraining.com

http://www.socstraining.com

http://www.wpvprevention.com

http://www.psti-elearning.com

Active Shooter: How To Respond.
http://www.alerts.si.edu/docs/DHS_ActiveShooterBook.pdf

Active Shooter: Recommendations and Analysis for Risk Mitigation.
http://www.nypdshield.org/public/SiteFiles/documents/ActiveShooter.pdf

ASIS International Active Shooter resource page.
http://www.asisonline.org/education/activeShooter.xml

FEMA EMI IS-907 - Active Shooter: What You Can Do.
http://training.fema.gov/EMIWeb/IS/is907.asp

https://en.wikipedia.org/wiki/Active_shooter

https://www.aims.edu/about/departments/safety/training/active_shooter.pdf

Run, Hide, Fight www.readyhoustontx.gov

http://www.aig.com/content/dam/aig/america-canada/us/documents/business/industry/the-5-stages-of-an-active-shooter-brochure.pdf

http://alerts.si.edu/docs/DHS_ActiveShooterBook.pdf

http://www.dontnamethem.org/

https://en.wikipedia.org/wiki/Sandy_Hook_Elementary_School_shooting

https://en.wikipedia.org/wiki/Virginia_Tech_shooting

https://en.wikipedia.org/wiki/2012_Aurora_shooting

https://en.wikipedia.org/wiki/2011_Tucson_shooting

https://info.publicintelligence.net/DHS-FBI-ActiveShooters.pdf

http://www.securitymagazine.com/articles/83930-fbi-4-percent-of-active-shooters-since-2002-were-female

https://www.fbi.gov/file-repository/activeshooterincidentsus_2014-2015.pdf/view

https://en.wikipedia.org/wiki/2011_Seal_Beach_shooting

https://en.wikipedia.org/wiki/Colorado_Springs_Planned_Parenthood_shooting

http://publicsafety.med.miami.edu/emergencies-what-to-do/emergency-active-shooter

http://www.patc.com/weeklyarticles/print/active-shooter-08.pdf

http://controversialtimes.com/issues/constitutional-rights/12-times-mass-shootings-were-stopped-by-good-guys-with-guns/

https://www.washingtonpost.com/news/volokh-conspiracy/wp/2015/10/03/do-civilians-with-guns-ever-stop-mass-shootings/?utm_term=.8373a89601ea

http://concealednation.org/2015/10/here-are-5-times-concealed-carriers-have-stopped-mass-shootings/

http://www.personaldefenseworld.com/2015/03/10-cases-where-an-armed-citizen-took-down-an-active-shooter/

http://www.policemag.com/channel/patrol/news/2016/02/26/video-kansas-active-shooter-kills-3-wounds-14-before-being-stopped-by-single-heroic-officer.aspx

http://www.ems1.com/mass-casualty-incidents-mci/articles/1633232-EMS-operations-during-an-active-shooter-incident/

https://www.usfa.fema.gov/downloads/pdf/publications/active_shooter_guide.pdf

U.S. Secret Service, National Threat Assessment Center.
https://www.secretservice.gov/protection/ntac/

Federal Bureau of Investigation.
https://www.fbi.gov/about/partnerships/office---of---partner---
    engagement/active---shooter---resources

J. Pete Blair and Katherine W. Schweit, A Study of Active Shooter
Incidents, 2000-2013, (Texas State University, FBI, 2014),
https://www.fbi.gov/file-repository/active-shooter-study-2000-2013-
1.pdf/view

Katherine W. Schweit, Active Shooter Incidents in the United States
in 2014 and 2015, (FBI, 2016), https://www.fbi.gov/file-
repository/activeshooterincidentsus_
2014-2015.pdf/view

Everytown for Gun Safety, Analysis of Recent Mass Shootings, (2016), https://everytownresearch.org/documents/2015/09/analysismasssho otings.pdf; Appendix, http://everytownresearch.org/ documents/2015/10/mass-shootings-analysis-appendix.pdf

Mother Jones, "U.S. Mass Shootings, 1982-2016" (2016), www. motherjones.com/politics/2012/12/mass-shootings-mother-jones-full-data

Melissa Jeltsen, "We're Missing the Big Picture on Mass Shootings." Huffington Post (Sept. 15, 2015), www.huffingtonpost.com/entry/massshootings-domestic-violence-women_us_55d3806ce4b07addcb44542a

https://leb.fbi.gov/articles/featured-articles/addressing-the-problem-of-the-active-shooter

https://www.dhs.gov/xlibrary/assets/active_shooter_booklet.pdf

https://www.fbi.gov/file-repository/active-shooter-incidents-us-2016-2017.pdf/view

https://www.fbi.gov/about/partnerships/office-of-partner-engagement/active-shooter-resources

https://www.fbi.gov/file.../pre-attack-behaviors-of-active-shooters-in-us-2000-2013.

https://www.washingtonpost.com/graphics/2018/national/mass-shootings-in-america/?noredirect=on&utm_term=.35ae4b2837e4

https://www.bleedingcontrol.org/

https://www.dhs.gov/stopthebleed

https://www.dhs.gov/see-something-say-something

https://www.ems.gov/projects/stop-the-bleed.html

http://www.hasc.org/active-shooter-drill-resources

https://www.fbi.gov/file-repository/active-shooter-incidents-in-the-us-2019-042820.pdf/view

https://www.fbi.gov/file-repository/making-prevention-a-reality.pdf/view

https://www.gunviolencearchive.org/

SURVIVE AN ACTIVE SHOOTER

The AVADE® Active Shooter Training Program Is Designed to Increase Your **Awareness, Preparedness,** and **Responses** for Extreme Violence

ESCAPE | RUN

HIDE | & COVER IN PLACE

ATTACK | THE ATTACKER

1 **Escape (Run)** if Safe to Do So!

2 **Hide & Cover** in Place if You Can't Escape

3 **Alert (911) Authorities** | Police & Armed Security

4 **Lock Doors** in Your Immediate Area

5 Place Barriers & Remain **Absolutely Quiet**

6 If Escape is Not Possible & Danger is Imminent, **Attack (FIGHT) the Attacker**

7 When Law Enforcement Arrives, **Be Submissive, Expose Your Palms, & Do What They Tell You to Do**

 Active Shooter Defined:
The FBI defines an **Active Shooter** as *one or more individuals actively engaged in killing or attempting to kill people in a populated area.* Implicit in this definition is the shooter's use of **one** or **more firearms.**

Education, Prevention, and Mitigation for *Violence in the Workplace*
1.866.773.7763 · personalsafetytraining.com · avadetraining.com
© Personal Safety Training Inc. | AVADE® Training

TRAINING COURSES FOR YOU AND YOUR AGENCY

The only way to deal with conflict and avoid violence of any type is through awareness, vigilance, avoidance, defensive training, and escape planning."

PSTI, specializes in nationally recognized training programs that empower individuals, increase confidence, and promote proactive preventative solutions. OSHA, Labor & Industries, Joint Commission, State WPV Laws, and the Dept. of Health all recognize that programs like PSTIs are excellent preventive measures to reduce crime, violence, and aggression in the workplace.

www.PersonalSafetyTraining.com

PSTI Offers
On-Site Training (We will come to you!) No need to send staff away for training. PSTI will come to your place of business and train your staff.

Train-the-Trainer (Instructor Seminars)
The most cost-effective way to implement PSTI training courses for your organization. We can come to you for instructor courses, or you can send staff to one of our upcoming seminars.

Combo Classes
Combination classes are where basic training and instructor training are combined during on-site training. It is a great way to introduce PSTI training with our initial instruction and then continue on with your own instructors.

E-Learning
Are you looking for a training solution to integrate a workplace violence prevention program in order to meet compliance standards for both State and Federal guidelines? The AVADE® E-learning programs offer a great solution to give your staff an introductory yet comprehensive training program that can be completed as needed.

About Us

Personal Safety Training Inc. is committed to providing the finest level of training and service to you and your employees. Whether you are an individual or represent an agency, we have the Basic and Instructor Course Certifications that YOU need.

Contact Us

Personal Safety Training, Inc.
P.O. Box 2957, Coeur d' Alene, ID 83816
(208) 664-5551—Fax (208) 664-5556
www.personalsafetytraining.com

Multiple training options for your organization:

- 2 hr. Intro Courses

- 1/2 Day Training Sessions

- One Day Classes

- Two Day Classes

- Train-the-Trainer (Instructor Classes)

PSTI serves a variety of industries:

Healthcare – Corporate - Security – Gaming - Churches

TRAINING COURSES FOR YOU AND YOUR AGENCY

SOCS® (Safety Oriented Customer Service)

SOCS® training teaches staff how to identify and provide great customer service while maintaining safety in the workplace. The core concept of the training is to be able to provide excellent service without having to think about it. Creating habits, skills and taking action for exceptional customer service is the goal of the SOCS® training program. www.SOCStraining.com

AVADE® DTS™ (Defensive Tactics System)
The DTS™ training program covers basic defensive tactics, control techniques, and defensive interventions. The course includes stance, movement, escort techniques, take-downs, defensive blocking, active defense skills, weapon retention, handcuffing, post-incident response and documentation, and much much more. www.dts-training.com

AVADE® Personal Safety Training
Buy the ultimate book and training on HOW to keep you and your family safe. Call us for training. The training program is designed to increase your overall safety in all environments. The curriculum is based on David Fowler's book, Be Safe Not Sorry—the Art and Science of keeping YOU and your family safe from crime and violence.

AVADE® Workplace Violence Prevention
The Workplace Violence Prevention Training is offered as a Basic and Instructor level course for private corporations, healthcare, security companies' and any agency wanting to educate, prevent and mitigate the risk of violence to their employees. www.avadetraining.com

AVADE® Pepper Spray Defense™ Training
Tactical and Practical concepts of when and how to use pepper spray in a variety of environmental situations. Aerosol Pepper is a great less-than-lethal control and defense option for agencies that encounter violence and aggression. www.pepperspraydefense-training.com

AVADE® Defense Baton™ Training
Training in the use of an expandable baton, straight stick, or riot control baton. Techniques and topics in this training include: vulnerable areas of the body, stance, movement, blocks, control holds, counter techniques, draws, and retention techniques. www.defensebaton.com

AVADE® Handcuffing Tactics™

Training in the use of plastic, chain, or hinged handcuffs. Standing, kneeling, and prone handcuffing techniques are covered. In this training course, you will also learn DT fundamentals, proper positioning, nomenclature, risk factors, and post-incident response and documentation. www.handcuffingtactics.com

AVADE® HDTS™ (Healthcare Defensive Tactics System)

The HDTS™ training program for healthcare covers basic defensive tactics, control techniques, and defensive interventions. The course includes stance, movement, escort techniques, take-downs, team intervention, defensive blocking, active defense skills, weapon retention, patient restraint techniques, post-incident response and documentation, and much much more. www.hdts-training.com

AVADE® SIRS™ (Safety Incident Reporting System)

A training program that teaches officers how to effectively and intelligently write safety incident reports. Documentation of security incidents is absolutely critical to your agency's ability to track and trend, reduce liability, and share vital information. If you're like most agencies–you know that proper, structured, effective, and reliable reports save time and money and allow you to track incidents and reduce liability risk. www.sirs-training.com

AVADE® Active Shooter

The AVADE® Active Shooter training is designed to increase awareness, preparedness, and response to extreme violence. The philosophy of education, prevention, and mitigation is the cornerstone of this training program. www.avadeactiveshooter.com

AVADE® Violence in the Workplace (versions I, II, and III)

Buy the book on HOW to be safe in the workplace. This is the text based on the AVADE® training system. Can't come to a class; at least get the book! The knowledge contained in these pages will teach YOU awareness, vigilance, avoidance, defensive interventions, and escape strategies for your place of business.

Made in the USA
Monee, IL
30 April 2023

32625944R00079